Remember Me

*For Michele Barbotto,
in memory of the Potentissima, of Bar Verde
and everything that death has left here*

Remember Me

Memory and Forgetting in the Digital Age

Davide Sisto

Translated by Alice Kilgarriff

polity

Originally published in Italian as *Ricordati di me: La rivoluzione digitale tra memoria e oblio* © 2020 Bollati Boringhieri editore, Torino

This English edition © Polity Press, 2021

The translation of this work has been funded by SEPS Segretariato Europeo per le Pubblicazioni Scientifiche

Via Val d'Aposa 7 – 40123 Bologna – Italy
seps@seps.it – www.seps.it

Polity Press
65 Bridge Street
Cambridge CB2 1UR, UK

Polity Press
101 Station Landing
Suite 300
Medford, MA 02155, USA

ISBN-13: 978-1-5095-4503-2 (hardback)
ISBN-13: 978-1-5095-4504-9 (paperback)

A catalogue record for this book is available from the British Library.

Typeset in 10.5 on 12 Sabon
by Fakenham Prepress Solutions, Fakenham, Norfolk NR21 8NL
Printed and bound in Great Britain by Short Run Press

The publisher has used its best endeavours to ensure that the URLs for external websites referred to in this book are correct and active at the time of going to press. However, the publisher has no responsibility for the websites and can make no guarantee that a site will remain live or that the content is or will remain appropriate.

Every effort has been made to trace all copyright holders, but if any have been overlooked the publisher will be pleased to include any necessary credits in any subsequent reprint or edition.

For further information on Polity, visit our website: politybooks.com

Contents

Acknowledgements

Writing a book on memory and memories has, for me, been a titanic endeavour. I do not have an easy relationship with 'looking back', as it always leaves me with a melancholy sense of loss. This forces upon me the need always to look ahead and to recognize the importance of dying and being forgotten. However, as incoherence tends to win out over coherence, looking back is the central issue of this book which, having been written in order to be published and read, reveals the author's implicit desire to leave his mark.

I would like, first and foremost, to offer my most heartfelt thanks to Roberto Gilodi, Michele Luzzatto, Flavia Abbinante, Elena Cassarotto and the publishing house Bollati Boringhieri for having given me the opportunity to write this book.

I would also like to thank all of those with whom I share, each and every day, the objective of bringing the discourse on death back into the public space in order to limit the negative effects of its social and cultural repression: Marina Sozzi and the blog *Si può dire morte*; Ines Testoni and the Masters in *Death Studies and the End of Life* at the University of Padua; Ana Cristina Vargas, Gisella Gramaglia and Fondazione Ariodante Fabretti in Turin; Maria Angela Gelati and *Il Rumore del Lutto* in Parma; Massimiliano Cruciani and *Zero*

K in Carpi; Laura Campanello and the Death Cafè in Merate; Alice Spiga and the SO.CREM. in Bologna.

I would also like to thank everyone who has shown interest and enthusiasm for *Online Afterlives*, giving me the possibility of discussing the book's themes throughout Italy. I will cherish the memories of moving experiences I have had from North to South over the last year and a half. I am truly grateful to those splendid individuals whom I have had the opportunity to meet from time to time.

I would also like to thank Ade Zeno, friend and companion in never-ending thanatological adventures; Valentino Farina, in memory of past times; and Dedalo Bosio, the Splunge cited in this book. Finally, I would like to thank Lorenza Castella, because she doesn't read my books and therefore will never know she has been thanked.

The final and most important mentions go to Nello and Silvana, and to my irreplaceable Roberta, so involved in this book (poor her!) that she dreamed about it at night. May many *pasticcini al pistacchio* atone for my sins.

Introduction
Social Networks and Looking Back

The Past is Just a Story We Tell Our Followers

The past is just a story we tell ourselves. These are the words Samantha, the OS1 operating system and the protagonist in Spike Jonze's film *Her*, uses to console Theodore Twombly, the man who constantly imagines he is talking to his ex-wife, Catherine. He picks up on old, never forgotten conversations and uses hindsight to construct justifications he was unable to give when the woman, before leaving him, pointed out his repeated failings. The past does not really exist. This point is made unremittingly by Jonathan Gottschall in his book *The Storytelling Animal*: though it may have actually happened, the way in which we present it makes it seem like nothing more than 'a mental simulation'. Our memories are not perfect recordings of what actually happened but reconstructions, and most of their details are unreliable.[1] This is probably what pushed Desmond Morris to take such a radical step following the death of the woman with whom he had lived for sixty-six years, getting rid of all the physical memories that made his grief unbearable. As Aleida Assmann observes, 'By erasing a mark, the survival of a person or an event in the memory of those who come after becomes as impossible as the discovery of a crime.'[2] Therefore, the

British zoologist asked himself, why not eliminate *all* traces? The thousands of books, paintings and antiques bought with his wife over the course of more than half a century of marriage, those simple utensils (a teacup, for example) that symbolically contain the most normal daily gestures of a shared life, along with photographs, and even a whole house. The house represents 'a deposit, that exists both physically and within us, of memories that are still shared', it is 'the final bulwark of a time painstakingly removed [...] from the unrelenting progression of loss, from the painful dissipation of living worlds'.[3] Morris follows this rule: if you leave me, I'll erase you.

Theodore Twombly in cinematic fiction, and Desmond Morris in real life, share the same fate: the end of the world in its totality, to borrow a famous expression from Jacques Derrida. Both the end of a sentimental relationship and the death of a loved one suddenly erase the physical presence to which we are bound, along with everything that had been shared both materially and emotionally up until that moment. Twombly and Morris suddenly find themselves at the starting point of their own lives, as if every experience up to that moment had been erased. The only thing posing any opposition to the end of the world in its totality is the spectral presence of the person who is no longer physically there, the transparent copy that proliferates in material and mental memories, remaining alive and kicking in their scattered remains. That copy, which according to Umberto Eco is relied upon by every human being who, aware of both their physical ('I'm going to die sooner or later') and mental weakness ('I'm sorry that I'm going to have to die'), finds proof of that soul's survival in the memory that remains of it.[4] In other words, both the death of a loved one and the end of a loving relationship determine the passage from identity to the *images* of identity that transform the absent into a collector's item, the bulwark against the memory's fragility at which one can direct their own enduring regrets.

The inevitable disconnect between the disappearance of the physical presence and the force of the spectral presence usually generates profound emotional unrest in the person left behind. The bitter knowledge of the end of the whole world is continually invoked by the eternal excess of its shadows and images, which make thoughts and objects that were once shared the exclusive inheritance of the person who is suffering. This is why, in cases where the grief is particularly unbearable, it can be useful to remember Samantha's suggestion: to view the past as a story we have told ourselves, breaking its suffocating bond with the present. Ghosts are kept at a safe distance, as per the approach taken by Desmond Morris, to avoid us becoming their prisoners, like Theodore Twombly. As Thomas Hobbes teaches us, if we set aside the passing of time, we have no way of distinguishing memory from imagination.[5] And, as Bertolt Brecht confirms, 'without the forgetfulness of night which washes away all traces', we would never find the strength to get up in the morning.[6]

Morris, however, has to reckon with a greater problem than Twombly: he is obliged to walk the fine line between his own sacrosanct need to forget and his dead wife's equally legitimate desire to be remembered.

So what happens when the past becomes a story that we not only tell ourselves but also our followers, *recording it* on social media profiles and online more generally?

If, traditionally, the house is the archetype of hybrid memory, filled as it is with the past in various areas of the domestic space and thus becoming an extreme stronghold of a time removed from the urgent rhythm of loss, our second home today is the online realm. To inhabit, Walter Benjamin explained, means 'to leave impressions'. This is confirmed by the invention of 'an abundance of covers and protectors, liners and cases [...] on which the traces of objects of everyday use are imprinted'.[7] In those countless online rooms, we are constantly recording, accumulating and preserving these marks in excessive quantities, creating digital deposits of our memories and delegating our own faltering memories to artificial tools. In comparison with the first house, the internet's front door is always ajar, if not wide open. *Sharing* has become one of its defining imperatives. As Kevin Kelly writes, it is also 'the world's largest copy machine' because it is continually updating, '[copying] every action, every character, every thought we

make while we ride upon it'.[8] It copies our own psycho-
physical presence, dematerializing it. It detaches myriad
digital I's from the biological I physically present in only
one location in the offline world, creating digital presences
that wander (more neurotic than carefree) throughout
all possible places in the web, leaving indelible marks
through an unbridled multiplication of their personal
and social identities. Human beings, historical constructs
whose contingency depends on continuous and ongoing
technological progress, have learned how to develop more
'informational souls'. Reciprocally connected within the
Infosphere, these souls occupy spaces in which there is no
distinction between natural individuals and artificial agents.
They reveal, therefore, a brand new virtue with regard to
'spiritual' souls, that of satisfying in equal measure the 'two
figures obsessed by immortality' referred to by Elias Canetti:
both the one that wants infinite continuity with time, and
the one that instead wishes to return periodically.[9] As we
find in inter-disciplinary studies on *Digital Death*,[10] these
technological spectres help our digital I's attain that eternal
life denied their biological twin, who remains exposed to
the whim of the Grim Reaper.

It follows that, unlike those objects held within domestic
walls, for the most part private, unique and rare specimens
(*physical* in the broad sense) that facilitate the choice
taken by Desmond Morris, the data accumulated in digital
deposits (written messages, photographic images, audiovisual
recordings, and so on) are difficult to erase. The fact that
these data are shared not only obviously means they are not
private, but also means they enjoy the gift of ubiquity and can
be multiplied infinitely. Some are shared voluntarily (in posts
left on social media profiles), some are shared unwittingly
(every trace a user leaves on a device while online), some are
shared by third parties (the problematic habit common to
parents of posting photographs of their underage children,
usually on Facebook). It can all exist autonomously and in
an indeterminate number of copies, occupying the internal
space of an equally unknown quantity of electronic devices
and online locations. Each of these devices and locations in
turn represents a privileged point of 24/7 access to digital
memories. The distinction between 'internal' and 'external'

has now become superfluous in comparison with historical eras in which, in the absence of digital technology, the house acted as the custodian of private memories, clearly marking the boundary between inside and outside.

So, while it is relatively easy to 'empty' material deposits once mourning has taken place, placing a protective barrier between the world that has come to an end and the world that must now be built, it is much more difficult (if not impossible) to do the same thing with digital deposits. Like the 'invisible cascade of skin cells'[11] that we leave in the streets of our cities, the collection of data, digital footprints and information recorded online that is constantly photocopied and to which we delegate our memories with increasing frequency, makes those ghosts that assail Twombly's mind at night increasingly pervasive and permanent, and render Morris' attempts to chase them out entirely in vain.

Today's world seems struck by an epidemic of memory that provides the past with the opportunity to free itself from the present's control. As it slowly becomes autonomous as an objective reality in its own right, the past overlaps with the present, imposing itself from one moment to the next. As a consequence, it is liberated from the spectrality attributed by those who, until now, have always thought of it as either nothing more than a story we tell ourselves or a mere simulation produced by the mind. And it is preparing to subvert the very rules that govern the way in which we remember and forget.

Facebook and Looking Back: #10YearChallenge, On This Day, Memories

Mark Zuckerberg, the man most responsible for the recent multiplication of our informational souls, was the first person to recognize the radical shift taking place in the way we remember and forget. Taking the positive aspects, he ignores Samantha's advice and chooses to favour total recall over oblivion. As Kenneth Goldsmith writes, 'Our archiving impulse arises as a way to ward off the chaos of overabundance.'[12] Zuckerberg takes this on board, transforming

Facebook from the most popular social network in the world to a technological memory chest, a gigantic digital archive capable of: (1) *conserving* data shared by its users over the years, constantly recreating and reshaping the relationship between the past and the present; (2) carefully *selecting* those memories using its algorithms; (3) *making* the documents and the digital footprints each one has left *easily accessible*. An interactive archive that, unlike a traditional one, preserves 'those traces and remains of the past that are not part of a culture of active memory'.[13] They are those biographical aspects of individual memory, ostensibly lacking any primary use for society, but at the same time capable of keeping our digital I perennially alive, reproduced in every single record that is made public.

Facebook's (ongoing) metamorphosis can be seen in the fact that *looking back* has been its most important feature for some time now. The perennial exhumation of what has happened within it seems to be a literal translation of the pathos and resonance Vilèm Flusser attributes to the internet in general, describing it as a 'way of loving our neighbour'.[14]

At some point towards the end of December, Facebook provides each of its two billion users with a video entitled 'Year in Review', alternating, in little more than a minute and against a strategically coloured background, the images and posts shared by the user over the past twelve months that received the highest number of likes and comments. Just like the brief videos created skilfully by online newspapers, in which the rapid succession of Juventus' most important goals illustrates their victory march towards their umpteenth championship title. Or those shown on television, in which a collage of a talk show's highlights is used to celebrate its season finale. At the end of the Facebook video, we read: 'Sometimes, looking back helps us remember what matters most. Thanks for being here.'

Anything but improvised, this 'looking back' exists all year round within standalone initiatives such as the #10YearChallenge. All it took was a simple hashtag, which went viral in a matter of minutes in January 2019, to convince millions of Facebook users to post photos to their Walls, publicly comparing a current photo of themselves to one taken ten years earlier. The most cynical of observers interpreted this challenge as yet another cunning strategy to obtain substantial amounts of personal data and images with which to train facial recognition algorithms. The fact remains that beyond any possible hidden agendas, millions of people dug up personal photos from 2009 and wallowed in collective nostalgia for a good few days. This took the form of a self-satisfied longing for an imagined, and distant, golden age: a decade before, yes, but still in reach. A time that, when observed with the disenchantment typical of the present, does not include the often hastily made choices taken over the years, nor the disappointments into which once-held ideals have since mutated, nor the inevitable failures, and nor does it see, on a much more basic level, the wrinkles and white hairs as merciless markers of Chronos' insensitivity. This is a nostalgic wallowing into which Instagram also plays, becoming involved in the challenge and therefore party to the onslaught of millions of images accompanied by the same hashtag. The initiative takes on further significance if we remember that the majority of personal events that have taken place over the last decade, events this explicitly invokes, have been documented on a daily basis on the above-mentioned social networks.

Since late spring 2015, the retrospective gaze has become a daily protagonist thanks to the On This Day feature. 'You have a new memory' is the notification text that celebrates this ritual, automatically directing our digital devices to a post, video or photograph shared on Facebook (or one in which we have been tagged) on the same day as it occurred in the past. Apart from recurring or historical events, On This Day rhapsodically revives biographical events or personal stories using algorithms. Initially, this 'looking back' is only visible to the user, who is then free to decide whether or not to share (and therefore make current) the memory with all of their followers. If the user chooses to share the post, they can leave it as it is or they can modify it partially with a comment that provides context for the present.

Alternatively, they can relive these moments in a private way or eliminate them completely. The stated aim of On This Day is to connect the present to nostalgia, sparking new debate between users that aims to resurrect that which, once it has happened, should, in theory, be lost forever.

In other words, it tends towards just one of the two paths that, according to Johann Jakob Bachofen, characterize any act of recognition: not the long, slow, hard path of rational reconstruction, but the shortcut 'that is travelled with the power and velocity of electricity, the road of the imagination that suddenly grasps the truth, in a split second, the moment it comes into contact with archaeological remains without relating it to anything'.[15] Suddenly, past and present find themselves mixed together, making it particularly difficult to distinguish clearly between the two. We see this when a user chooses an old photo as their current profile picture. The comments written by followers on the day in which it was originally shared merge with those written later, causing them to become confused. More often than not the consequences of this are equally odd. For example, it could be that beneath the image of a woman are comments from both her current husband and her ex (unless he has been blocked), both of which refer to her as if she were their wife. Only a close inspection of the date in which the post was originally shared by the reader avoids any suspicion of polygamy.

On 13 June 2018 there was a passage from On This Day to Memories that was as decisive as it was emblematic. While On This Day offered the user a single post shared on the same date of a different year, Memories (www.facebook.com/memories) is a parallel timeline included in the Explore section, where all the posts shared on each day of all past years are collated. Memories wholeheartedly adopt 'the simple mystery of concomitance' that Roland Barthes attributes to photography, believing the date the photo was taken to be an integral part of its whole. The date does not denote a style, but 'it makes me lift my head, allows me to compute life, death, the inexorable extinction of the generations'.[16] The Memories section does not perhaps aspire to such heights. However, its objective is clear from the moment in which it greets us with the words: 'We hope that you enjoy *looking back* on your memories on Facebook, from the most recent memories to those long ago' [my italics]. Scrolling back through the wall, we find everything we have shared on any given day laid out in descending order. On 25 February 2019, I click on Memories and immediately discover that

I shared two photographs on the same day in 2018: one depicting my city, Turin, blanketed in snow by the arrival in Italy of the freezing Siberian wind named 'Burian' by enthusiastic meteorologists, and the other showing a ticket for the Nirvana concert I went to as a teenager on 25 February 1994 in Milan, in the venue that used to be called the Palatrussardi. Ticket number: 8211. Cost: 32,000 lire. That was the Seattle grunge band's penultimate ever concert, as Kurt Cobain committed suicide just a month and half later. This event was therefore relevant from both a personal perspective and an historical one. Moving down the page, I re-read two of my posts: the first, dated 25 February 2017, refers to the faltering political situation in Italy at that precise moment, while the second, dated 25 February 2016, contains a number of personal considerations of a vaguely existential nature (not purposefully so) on the passing of time. The subject shared with my followers the previous year was somewhat lighter: a piece of dark chocolate eaten at 1am. Going even further back, I discover that in 2013, a friend who lives in Finland had written a post on my wall notifying me he was going to a heavy metal concert, knowing how much of a fan I am. In 2012, I was tagged by another friend after an evening spent in San Salvario, an area of Turin famous for its nightlife. And so on, all the way to my first ever 25 February post on Facebook: that from 2009. Once this journey back through the personal memories of that day has come to an end, close friendships from past years are listed alongside special videos or collages celebrating new contacts. Significant events from the user's personal life are then listed, regardless of whether or not they happened that day: the anniversary of a wedding or a graduation, or the start of a new job. The 'looking back' ends with a succinct: 'That's all for today.' Anyone can go into Memories to re-share one or more of these memories, making them current in the same way as On This Day. When there are no posts shared on that day, Facebook points this out and invites the user to check the next day or perhaps activate specific notifications for memories so that none are missed.

The invention of the Memories section, according to Facebook's product manager, Oren Hod, is justified by the fact that around ninety million people use On This Day each day, using the social network to relive experiences that are long gone, and therefore revive their own past. As a consequence, the creation of Memories provides all users with a dedicated place for their personal memories that allows them to consult these easily and intuitively without having to scroll through the hundreds or thousands of posts shared over the years. It would seem, then, that as far as ninety million people are concerned, it is not enough simply to tell the story of their past to themselves.

These numbers allow us to predict that Facebook in a not-too-distant future will create its own universal database of memories, which could be consulted using a simple single-word search. In this way Facebook will make definitive use of key word indexing (introduced in 2013) with a view to analysing our shared posts, looking for correlations, recurrent themes and anomalies in the lives recorded within it. Despite the inherent difficulty posed by managing such a vast level of content, this prediction is corroborated by the presence of a system that allows every user to make single searches by year, month and day within their own profile and those of their contacts. All they need to do is head to the 'Activity Log' section and select the year and month of interest, highlighting the shared posts, images and links to be recovered. In addition to this there is a 'Stories' archive that is easy to search and that can be downloaded onto the user's computer. The 'Stories', used by both Facebook and Instagram, initially seem to prove Samantha right. They are, indeed, temporary ways of sharing photographs, videos and written texts. They stay visible for 24 hours after which time they delete themselves, just as happens with Snapchat content. Their objective is the creation of a kind of live streaming of our very existence, meaning immediacy, instantaneousness and the avoidance of recording are their fundamental prerogatives. However, the collective desire to preserve them and revive them whenever we wish has pushed those in charge at Facebook and Instagram to create a specific space that overwhelmingly downsizes the *carpe diem* inherent in these platforms.

Facebook even allows users to download the entirety of the digital life they have lived within its labyrinthine workings. If you visit the profile section on information, accessed from the general Settings page, you find a way of archiving all that content on your own computer: posts, photos, video, likes and reaction, friends, stories, messages, groups and so on. The download can include both single publications, once the type of information and desired timeframe have been selected, and the entire collection of documents. It is possible to choose between a HTML format, which is easier to view, and the JSON format that allows for another service to import the data immediately. This download, which involves a substantial amount of time for those profiles that have been particularly active over the years, is password-protected and only the account user is able to access it. It also only exists for a limited amount of time before it is automatically deleted. Alternatively, in the case of the user's death (though only if they have previously given permission) this can be accessed by a legacy contact. Once the friend's death has been certified, the legacy contact can carry out the download and archive a copy of the deceased's profile and all its contents (excluding private messages) on their own computer. Thus, the digital memory carefully constructed by the deceased during their time on Zuckerberg's social network will be preserved forever.

From the video celebrating the year that is about to end, to impromptu hashtags such as #10YearChallenge, to On This Day and Memories, arriving at the copy in a single file of all of your digital memories produced on Facebook over the years, Zuckerberg seems to make his own, albeit optimistically, the unnerving thought expressed by Mark Fisher: 'in conditions of *digital recall* loss is itself lost'.[17] Thanks to digital technology, the recollections *buried* in our memory today have the possibility of being *disinterred* at any moment in our daily life and *brought back to life*, once more achieving that same actuality that had characterized them when they had first been experienced.

This book, developing the reflections on Digital Death made in *Online Afterlives*, aims to analyse the philosophical consequences of this digital unearthing of memories for our way of remembering and forgetting, shining a light on the parallel effects of the past's gradual emancipation from control by the present. In order to do this, it is necessary first to revisit those fundamental stages in the journey that has led, in less than twenty years, to the metamorphosis of social networks such as Facebook into technological memory chests and digital archives.

1

From Social Networks to Digital Archives

The Twenty Days of Turin: *Facebook in 1977*

Facebook's gradual metamorphosis from social network to colossal digital archive, as evidenced by initiatives like On This Day and Memories, is mostly due to its age: years have passed since Facebook first appeared on 4 February 2004 in Harvard. It is inevitable, then, that its objectives have changed since it was first invented. Having initially created Facebook as an electronic version of the traditional school yearbook, Zuckerberg gave shape to the three conjoined actions that generally define social networks: the construction of a public or semi-public profile within a closed system, the articulation of a list of other users with whom a connection is made, and the possibility of seeing and moving through the list of connections created by other people signed up to the same system. Three conjoined actions that allow us to use a web-based service that is capable of radically repositioning the individual within the public space: from a 'detail' and a 'small, interchangeable cog in the great mechanism of sociality' to the 'centre of one's own network of relationships'.[1]

This repositioning, often held to be the fundamental cause of the shift from web 1.0 to web 2.0, is closely associated with Facebook. Its invention seems to have irrefutably determined a new beginning in humanity's cultural history, marking the beginning of Silicon Valley's season of psychopathology (a term coined by Éric Sadin with a distinctly apocalyptic emphasis), with Facebook deemed the main culprit for spreading that individualistic sentiment of egocentric omnipotence throughout the world.[2] In reality, all Zuckerberg does is bring together, with cunning and foresight, those single dispersive intuitions which, over the course of the last four decades, have accompanied the dominance of gradual technological innovation. Rather than actually beginning the era of the social network, Facebook marks a point of no return, accelerating the process of splitting the unique biological I into many digital I's and favouring the progressive development of our informational souls, fed to the point of indigestion on incalculable quantities of data. To understand my motivation for this statement we must make a leap backwards in time to 1977, the year in which eclectic author Giorgio De Maria published his novel *The Twenty Days of Turin* (*Le venti giornate di Torino*) to widespread indifference.

Only six years had passed since electronic engineer Roy Tomlinson sent his 'QWERTYUIOP' message from one computer to another using the Arpanet network, using the @ sign for the first time as a means of separating the user from the domain, which acts as a post box. An aside: a trick of fate means that we will always associate the first sequence of letters on a computer keyboard, from left to right, with the mother of the 270 billion emails that are written and sent each day (according to figures published by *Esquire* in 2018), multiplying the chaos of overabundance so dear to Goldsmith. At this time, De Maria, employed at Italian state broadcaster RAI and Fiat, as well as being a theatre critic, television screenwriter, accomplished pianist, dramaturg and much more, develops (albeit unwittingly) a description of what would become Facebook forty years later. In his story, set in an obsessively dark Turin, he imagines the existence of a Library, situated in the charitable institute of the St Cottolengo Little House of Divine Providence, in which every citizen can leave their own autobiographical narrative filled with personal anecdotes and subjective reflection on their everyday lives. At the same time, it is possible to read (upon payment) the thoughts left by other users. Created by young men supported (it says) by national and international organizations of considerable importance, the library is frequented by more than five hundred thousand people. De Maria writes, 'It was presented as a good cause, created in the hope of encouraging people to be more open with one another.'[3] The Library's creators are not interested in literary fiction but authentic documents capable of reflecting 'the real spirit of the people' that 'could rightly [be called] *popular subjects*':[4] summaries of intimate problems with constipation, admissions of wins on the pools, existential cogitations. For three hundred lire one can access texts by others, for six hundred one has the opportunity to learn the names and surnames of the authors, and for three thousand lire one's own manuscript will be accepted. De Maria observes how entire families, each member unaware of the others, go to this Library to mind other people's business, sifting through each room in search of skeletons in the cupboard. He also proves how the accumulation of personal texts facilitates the reconstruction of many historical events of the time. However, these autobiographical narratives do not necessarily conform to an objective truth:

> The pen could scribble freely whatever the spirit dictated. And once it started, it was hard to stop! The prospect of 'being read' quivered in the distance like an enchanting mirage – a mirage as real, nonetheless, as the 'realities' that were written down. I will give myself to you, you will give yourself to me: on these very human foundations, the future exchange would happen.[5]

A substantial number of citizens are reticent to write, limiting themselves to reading other people's reflections and trying to establish some kind of communication with the unknown authors, once they have obtained their personal data from the Library. The reflections consigned to the Library often degenerate into madness or furious outbursts hidden behind an apparent normality. Each entry reveals personal characteristics that are antithetical to the way the individual appears in society, permeated with passive-aggressive behaviour, between 'cries of fury and pain in relentless successions, fragments of sentences and pleas addressed to God-knows-who'.[6] It is no coincidence that the Library's average visitor is 'a shy individual, ready to explore the limits of his own loneliness and to weigh others down with it'.[7]

In a novel written in 1977, De Maria did in fact imagine and tell a story about what we know today as Facebook, in which visiting this particular Library has disturbing and horrific effects. *I will give myself to you, you will give yourself to me*, with all of the narcissistic degeneration this entails: from the omnipresent fake news to primordial forms of *shitstorms* produced by anonymous haters, slaves to their own 'inner troll'. Particularly striking is the description of the manuscripts that, 'conceived in a spirit of pure malice', make fun of the curve in an old woman's spine, a woman without husband or children. A description that anticipates by forty-one years that of the 'inner troll' (a malevolent troublemaker that intervenes in virtual interactions in a provocative, offensive and thoughtless way) given by Jaron Lanier as one of the ten reasons why we should immediately delete all of our social media accounts.[8] At the same time, today's reader cannot help but be struck by the nexus between obsessively visiting the Library, the development of a reciprocal spying network, and the outbreak of a collective insomnia, which, as the events recounted in the novel degenerate, highlights aspects that are very familiar to all those using social networks today: 'You couldn't leave the house any more, take a tram, visit a public place, without sensing the leer of somebody who wanted you to believe he'd soaked up all your deepest secrets. If I'd left any of *my* confessions in that place, I'd probably have lost sleep too.'[9]

The incredible similarity between the Library and Facebook has led to the posthumous rediscovery of *The Twenty Days of Turin*. Shortly after De Maria's death in 2009 due to severe mental health problems, Australian writer and critic Ramon Glazov discovered the novel by accident and was bowled over by it, deciding to translate it into English. In 2017 the book was published in the United States by W.W. Norton & Company to great critical and public acclaim. In the pages of the *New York Times*, Jeff VanderMeer, one of the main exponents of the modern New Weird genre praises

De Maria's sensational foresight. This was followed a few months later by a new Italian edition, published by Frassinelli Editore, aimed at promoting a book that had been unfairly ignored in Italy at the time.

Though De Maria's intuition is surprising, *The Twenty Days of Turin* is a novel written within a social and cultural context in which the first, sporadic forms of telematic communication immediately reveal an irrepressible human desire: the creation of social networking processes that, by making the varyingly authentic biographies of single individuals public, allow for long-distance relationships in which physical presence is latent or intentionally not sought out. Almost simultaneously with *The Twenty Days of Turin*, the typically social pact ('I will give myself to you' and in exchange, 'you will give yourself to me') finds its digital habitat (albeit a limited one) in the BBS (Bulletin Board System), which dates back to 1978, thanks to the work of Ward Christensen and Randy Suess. As Tatiana Bazzichelli explains, the BBS were based

> ... on the exchange of messages sent via modem and computer by several different users, in the spheres of different thematic areas of discussion. The computers of an amateur network were connected through telephone lines via modem and went on to form the 'hubs' of the network of many BBSes which, in turn, were connected. The messages circulated through the network mostly at night when the computers were predisposed to receive and send data, which travelled from node to node in a manner much slower than today.[10]

The BBSes, functioning both as mailing lists and online document archives, allowed the few users of the telematic network to send and, at the same time, receive both private messages through which they could maintain a relationship with a specific person, and public messages, which could be read by all those signed up to a particular collective discussion group. Once authenticated, the users interacted reciprocally, albeit asynchronously and with a speed directly proportional to the telematic systems in use at the time.[11] Though they did not yet play the specific role attributed to the Library by De Maria, the BBSes demonstrate how the development of digital technology follows the need to use them for inter-subjective relationships based on shared passions and ideas. The increase in their use coincided with the publication in 1981 of the first mail protocol (SMTP), which also sees a gradual increase in the use of electronic mail.

Naked in Front of the Computer: Social Networks in the 1990s

Tim Berners-Lee's historic invention in 1991 of the HTTP protocol (Hypertext Transfer Protocol), which allows for a hypertextual reading of documents and led to the development of the architecture for the World Wide Web, only just precedes the first SMS sent from a computer to a cell phone on the GSM Vodafone network: 'MERRY CHRISTMAS' written in upper case letters (and outrageously early) on 3 December 1992 by British engineer Neil Papworth. A year later in 1993, the first cell phone to cell phone SMS was sent thanks to the work of Finnish intern Riku Pihkonen at Nokia, at a time when the internet (only accessible through a frustratingly slow 56k modem) was synonymous with search engines such as Lycos and WebCrawler, browsers such as Netscape, and meeting places like Geocities.

But 1997 is the year that, only just preceding the invention of Google by Sergey Brin and Larry Page, the main objective of De Maria's library is taken seriously: *I will give myself to you, you will give yourself to me*. Most importantly, it is a year in which the neologism 'weblog' is used to describe a popular extension of online journalism, and, in Italy, Arianna and Virgilio stop simply being names and become the country's first search engine and directory, respectively. It is also a year in which an event of fundamental importance to humanity takes place: 11 June sees the birth of Sophie Kahn, daughter of American entrepreneur Philippe, but more importantly, a photograph is sent from a cell phone for the first time and shared through a collective network. Philippe immortalizes his daughter's birth with his digital camera. He downloads the image onto his mobile phone and uses the cell phone signal (there is no WiFi) to send it from his mobile phone to his home computer, which is connected to the internet. Finally, he sends the photographic image by email to his contacts. As Joan Fontcuberta observes, 11 June 1997 will forever be remembered as the day in which instant visual communication became reality. Just like Sophie.[12]

Curious though not coincidental is the fact that a week earlier (3 June, to be exact) *Album of the Year*, the sixth studio album by multi award-winning American crossover/ hard rock band Faith No More, was released. It is not so much the album's straight-forward title that interests us as the presence of the song, *Naked in Front of the Computer*, in the album's track list, the text of which denounces the habit (particularly widespread in the United States) of building long-distance interpersonal relationships exclusively through email. Mike Patton, Faith No More's lead singer and songwriter, sarcastically reworks Peter Steiner's famous cartoon, 'on the internet nobody knows you are a dog', published in 1993 in *The New Yorker*, imagining a scene considered ridiculous and entirely improbable at the time: an interpersonal relationship played out through a computer during which, given the absence of physical presence and so unbeknownst to the other, one of the two interlocutors is entirely in the nude. *They said it's normal. But they're keeping me dumb and hot*, is one of the song's central lines. Today's enemies of digital communications (Byung-Chul Han first and foremost) should, as a minimum, use *Naked in Front of the Computer* as the theme tune to each of their technophobic lessons.

1997 is also the year in which the first social network in history was officially born: SixDegrees.com, created by Andrew Weinreich, founder of Macroview Communication. Weinreich's aim was to put the 'six degrees of separation' theory into practice online, the first formulation of which can be found in the short story, *Chains*, written in 1929 by Hungarian author Frigyes Karinthy. According to this theory, anyone who wants to make contact with anyone else on the planet can do so through no more than five intermediaries. Each individual is connected to all others through a sequence of maximum six people. SixDegrees.com attempts to probe the veracity of this claim. As such, it offers its users a rudimentary digital platform that is more or less public, on which each can upload a photograph by which they can be identified and share their personal data (including their hobbies, job, etc.). Each user is obliged to provide the email addresses of two people they know in the 'six degrees group'. Once they have seen the list of those who have signed up, each user creates their own relationships, knowing that there are different degrees of separation: one degree of separation from those they know personally (friends and relatives), two degrees of separation from friends of friends (the so-called 'acquaintances' or simply subjects known to and frequented by their friends), three degrees of separation from subjects known by friends of their friends. In this way SixDegrees. com is able to maintain a certain level of control over the social networks within which each user is inserted, reproducing online the socio-economic groups to which they belong, while also organizing people according to their shared tastes. Indeed, anyone can contact another person using a series of filters (geographic location, hobby, gender, etc.), which allow users with similar interests to be grouped together. One hundred and fifty people signed up initially, invited via email by Weinreich himself. In three years, the number of users exceeds one million, a substantial number that led SixDegrees.com to develop a system for the sale of commercial products and the publication of job requests and offers within its existing system. On 7 December 1998, a journalist from *La Repubblica*, Fabio Santolini, wrote an article on SixDegrees.com, in which he voiced his suspicion 'that this huge population of internauts who search for friends, lovers or work connections on SixDegrees.com is actually useful to Mr Andrew Weinreich and his company, which finds itself in the possession of the names and emails of more than a million people. People whose tastes, preferences, inclinations (commercial ones included) he now knows. A goldmine for advertisers who can place highly effective and fruitful ad hoc advertising on the site.'[13] Sound familiar?

Over the course of the seven years separating the birth of SixDegrees and the invention of Facebook, numerous attempts were made to create the perfect social network, refining the various forms of self-representation for a global audience. Classmates.com proposes to make the nightmare of every sane adult a reality through its virtual reunion with classmates from school, who can be traced using a quick search through the page dedicated to your particular school. The service is still active today and has almost sixty million registered users. Clearly there aren't as many sane people as one might think. MakeOutClub.com in 1999 offers digital platforms for the creation of varied virtual communities based on shared interests. There is also AsianAvenue, BlackPlanet, MiGente, Rize.com, Tribe.net, each of which combine (according to their own specific prerogative) the need to create long-distance bonds with a desire to gain professional advantages in a time before LinkedIn hit upon its winning formula.

Among the most widely used pre-Facebook social networks, Friendster warrants a special mention. Used by several million subscribers from 2002, it quickly becomes one of the most visited websites in the world. What sets Friendster apart is not so much the offer of virtual spaces where users can share photographs and written messages once they have filled out a compulsory questionnaire that actually groups people according to their personal tastes, but its ability to anticipate the plot of the episode *Nosedive* from the acclaimed British television series, *Black Mirror*. *Nosedive* (2016) imagines a near future in which every person is given a score based on the reputation they have earned on social networks, and on which all daily activities depend, such as renting a house in a particularly prestigious residential area. Fourteen years earlier, Friendster was giving its users a popularity rating determined by the number of contacts they manage to accrue. The higher the number of contacts, the higher the popularity rating. Consequently, two years before the birth of Facebook, those using Friendster were already obsessed with broadening their own social network, trying to intercept the most popular users and even creating fake profiles of famous people or abstract entities (such as universities). The ultimate aim was to be seen by others as highly popular and, therefore, more attractive.

The same objective, albeit pursued using different strategies, leads to the birth and development of MySpace, the social network that comes closest to Facebook and which is (erroneously) considered the starting point for the era in which we are currently living. Accruing millions of subscribers in just a few years, MySpace allows each of them to create their own personal page on which to publicize their own activities, while simultaneously creating relationships with other people. It is primarily used by musicians to promote their upcoming albums. Indeed, they share their own music files and (in some cases) their first sporadic videos on YouTube, giving their fans the chance to communicate with them directly, though any communication within MySpace must be concise. This opportunity is, in theory, already offered by the band's official websites, though management often stops the kind of direct contact possible within MySpace. Although the association between MySpace and the birth of the era of social networks is erroneous, its capillary diffusion throughout the world leads to the broad acceptance of the opinion expressed by Michael S. Malone with regard to collective internet usage: 'Memory is now free, ubiquitous, and almost infinite; what matters now is not one's ownership of knowledge but one's skill at accessing it and analysing it.'[14]

The World Doubled: Reincarnation or the Cocaine of the Future?

MySpace was not 'humankind's definitive leap into the underworld', as Alessandro Baricco writes with excessive hyperbole in *The Game* (2018).[15] As we have seen, this leap into the digital underworld happened before MySpace through the progressive use of numerous social networks. However, these networks were not the only developments responsible for this transformation. Those left cold by online spaces such as SixDegrees.com and Friendster (used predominantly in the United States) used different environments hosted throughout the internet, such as personal blogs, forums on websites dedicated to specific topics (music, cinema, etc.), the communities created through the first electronic mail boxes, not to mention rudimentary versions of MSN Messenger and Skype. Those most clearly aware of this are those born between the late 1970s and the early 1980s, who are defined using a curious but emblematic neologism: Xennials. The term, deriving from a blend of Generation X and Millennials, broadly indicates a micro-generation of individuals destined to be 'stuck in the middle':

• Unlike Generation X, born between 1960 and 1975, their post-adolescence was literally overrun by the digital revolution.
• However, unlike Millennials or Generation Y, their childhoods and adolescence were spent entirely without the internet or electronic devices, apart from videogames and walkie-talkies, which were literally used like cell phones.

In other words, Xennials' formative years were spent exclusively within the offline world, accumulating only material memories such as letters, postcards, diaries, analogue photographs and so on, just like previous generations. Then suddenly, between the end of their adolescence and the beginning of their adult life, they saw their world double. And so, they quickly introduced their online copies, creating multiple versions of themselves through different avatars. To be clear, Xennials are those who began listening to music in early childhood on a Walkman using cassette tapes, always keeping a pencil handy in case the tape needed winding back. During their adolescence, they moved onto compact discs, (begrudgingly) spending what little money they had at their disposal on CDs to replace the tapes they'd consumed up until the day before. And they were the first, during their university years, to illegally download innumerable quantities of MP3 files from Napster, sharing them with unknown users and transposing the age-old practice of 'copying' tapes into the new online dimension. When Metallica became the first band to publicly raise the problem of digital piracy and copyright protection by suing Napster, the Xennials continued their essentially illegal activities, happily celebrating the birth of SoulSeek and its many descendants.

Online 'colonies' and 'pioneers' of the digital revolution is how Stefano Quintarelli describes them, while, according to Franco Berardi (Bifo), they are the first 'connective generation' enclosed in an environment defined by 'hyper-connectivity and hikikomori'.[16] Xennials experienced first hand both the opportunities and the problems inherent in the unprecedented attempt to found two different forms of relationships at the same time: the *traditional* kind, built in the offline world with one's own physical presence, and the *virtual* kind, resulting from the individuals congregating in the online world who, in absence of any geographical proximity and with their personal identities hidden behind eccentric nicknames, share the same interests. As such, they unwittingly passed through a transitional phase already predicted by Robert Pepperell in 1995 in his book *The Posthuman Condition*, as he recognized the progressive increase in the flow of information and digital data, signalling a passage from the certainties of the humanistic era, founded on anthropocentrism and the exclusively biological prerogatives of the human being, to the uncertainties of the post-human era, which finds the perfect opportunity to redefine the very contours of humanity in the hybridization of the biological and the technological. The 'posthuman condition' cited in the title of Pepperell's book, and influenced by the sci-fi imaginary of cyberpunk culture, does not aim to banally suggest *tout court* that humans have been surpassed, but instead announces the end of the gloriously self-centered human whose every action leads back to their biological self, convinced of their own infallibility, superiority and uniqueness. It is reductive to believe that the machines with which we have started to integrate are '*just* machines' rather than 'emerging forms of life' in perennial dialogue with us. Pepperell, in synch with the cybernetic theories of Norbert Wiener, proves how the progressive development of computers similar to human beings is counter-balanced by an inverse will to render human beings similar to computers.[17]

Around the same time *The Posthuman Condition* was published, Pierre Lévy asserted that the gradual familiarity that we begin to acquire with the (inherently vague) concept of 'virtual' represents, in terms of our biological presence, not so much a disincarnate alternative as a sort of reinvention or reincarnation: 'the body escapes itself, acquires new velocities, conquers new spaces. It overflows itself and changes technological exteriority or biological alterity into concrete subjectivity. By virtualizing itself, the body is multiplied. We create virtual organisms that enrich our sensible universe but do not cause us pain. Does this imply disembodiment?'[18] The 'disseminated body' is Antonio Caronia's response that, in keeping with Pepperell and Lévy, outlines the brand-new opportunities to connect (for example) our physical bodies to all kinds of devices, sensors or detectors that generate perfectly corresponding movements on avatars on computer screens. These technological innovations allow us to believe that the disseminated body is present 'every time that a real body can create "reality effects" through a technology even without its actual presence in a virtual dimension'.[19] Therefore, all bodies conceived as signifying surfaces and systems of communication grouped by their own unique features become 'disseminated': there is *transfer*. This term is used to indicate any activity that is aware that: 'no place, no encounter, no body is a point of arrival but a new point for exploration, and therefore, of departure', and as such 'a vital mechanism that strikes a direct hit on the frontier between the real and its representation'.[20] The new online dimension ultimately seems to represent an innovative and anarchic public space within which one's own desires, be they physical or mental, can be freely expressed, desires that are usually restrained or even censored through the rules and laws imposed by the offline dimension. Indeed, John Perry Barlow's 1996 *Declaration of the Independence of Cyberspace* opens with the following words:

> Governments of the Industrial World, you weary giants of flesh and steel, I come from Cyberspace, the new home of Mind. On behalf of the future, I ask you of the past to leave us alone. You are not welcome among us. You have no sovereignty where we gather.[21]

Cyberspace, lines of light aligned in the non-space of the mind, piles and constellations of data, according to the visionary description given by William Gibson in his book, *Neuromancer* (1984). ('The sky above the port was the colour of television, tuned to a dead channel')[22] is the proof that something is changing and that this something will entirely overwhelm humanity as we have historically known it, or has perhaps already done so without us realizing.

However, such a symptom is not viewed by all as positive and welcomed with open arms. On the contrary, there are those who interpret this as the destructive omen of a new and lethal future psychophysical addiction. The article, *Computer, cocaina del futuro* [*Computers: Cocaine of the Future*] written by journalist Michele De Russi and published on 25 January 1990 in Italian newspaper, *La Stampa*, is characteristic of this viewpoint: '

> Will the drug of the future be simulations created by computers, a made-to-measure electronic fiction that each of us can experience daily and that make us their protagonists? [...] Humans in the year 2000 will find themselves in an artificial reality in which they can take on almost divine functions, gaining even more gratification from this than they do from drugs. Through this they will be able to act out all of their fantasies, even forbidden ones, albeit in an ephemeral way. And there is the danger that they will become so dependent on this form of escape that the State will have to ban it, as has happened with narcotics.[23]

Faced with the choice between the dream of technological reincarnation and the threat of an as-yet unseen (not to mention 'narcotic') addiction, the Xennials initially opt for a third way of reading the situation that is in part closer to that of the sceptics: the perception of a gap that is difficult to bridge between the two dimensions, offline and online, into which the world has split itself. Unlike what is asserted by theorists of the posthuman condition, our adjustment to the new world cannot be described using the relationship the violinist creates with their instrument, in which the violin becomes a part of their body, broadening their range of expression and allowing it to be incorporated into their organism. But nor can it be described in terms of the more problematic relationship between the worker and the assembly line that, by generating a form of dependence, adheres to the fears expressed by sceptics: the workers make themselves an organ of the machine, they allow themselves to be incorporated into the machine's movements, mechanically adapting to the rules set by the cogs and wheels.[24]

The fact the online dimension can only be accessed when sitting at a static computer, and therefore subordinating the entrance to the new world to those tasks that must be carried out in the old one, ensured that the first online experiences took place with a clear differentiation between the dimensions of the 'real' and the 'virtual'. This differentiation was highlighted by numerous material difficulties that emerge every time there is an attempt to enter the new world, such as the excruciating waiting time in order to get online, the costly time-based tariffs that lead to a drastic parcelling out of time spent on the internet, the prohibitive cost of computers that reproduce the same social inequalities found in the old world, and so on.

The difference perceived between the two worlds, rather than producing a hybridization of the biological, the technological and the birth of those coveted disseminated bodies, undoubtedly creates a growing imbalance between the omnipotence promised by the new digital technologies that allow us to shape our subjective identities in any way we choose, and the sense of inadequacy brought about by our fragility and physical imperfections. The first experiments with an incorporeal existence mediated through screens turns them into new protective membranes through which it is possible to keep any form of holistic or complex sensorial interaction (which involves a vast amount of effort and annoyance) at a safe distance.[25] In other words, dominant among the first people to experience this doubled world is the consideration elaborated upon by Sherry Turkle in *Alone Together* (2011) – that the creation of one's own avatar is both a new way to explore oneself and a way to escape physical contact: 'You might have begun your online life in a spirit of compensation. If you were lonely and isolated, it seemed better than nothing [...]. Not surprisingly, people report feeling let down when they move from the virtual to the real world.'[26]

Blogs, Forums, Mailing Lists: A New Life in 56K

The search in the online world for what escapes us in the offline one, from desired reincarnations to threatening addictions, pushes the Xennials to capitalize on the little time at their disposal to access the new world. This gives rise to broad experimentation with every space offered by the web, mostly disoriented and disordered, starting with a kind of net-like individualism. From this comes an initial, timid accumulation of personal digital footprints, whose timid character is connected to the sense of reciprocal unfamiliarity experienced by both worlds, despite tens of thousands of virtual communities being formed over the course of the 1990s. This does not, however, take away from the fact that these first initial experiments within that copy of the physical world give rise to behaviour that, reiterated over time, would become an established custom, making possible the anthropological mutation that we will discuss shortly.

I personally experienced the first effects of this doubling of the world with my university friends between the end of the twentieth and the beginning of the twenty-first centuries, meeting both in the bars around the University of Turin, and in Splunge. Created by one of these friends and hosted on a domain (Vermario.com) that belonged to a shared acquaintance, Splunge was a blog that hosted daily discussions on popular culture, from indie music to arthouse cinema, from anything that at the time seemed *weird* or *eerie* in fiction and on television (still ignorant of the existence of Mark Fisher's theoretical interpretations) to news of the most extravagant and existential current events. Those commenting on the blog's content were not particularly numerous, a few dozen, hidden behind nicknames that despite making it difficult to automatically recognize the user personally were nevertheless forms of self-expression and ways of identifying one's own personal tastes (a passion for music, love for a book or videogame, and so on). One of the founding principles of personal online blogs was that of creating a community between people able to share anonymously their own philosophical reflections and describe their experiences, despite not knowing one another in the offline dimension. Hiding behind nicknames and, in particular, the fantastical invention of real-life experiences accentuated the distance between offline and online identities, much more so than happens now with the use of social networks in which everyone uses their own name and surname and tells their own personal stories (more or less). Furthermore, the connection between many personal blogs present on the same platform (Splinder at the beginning and later, Wordpress) generates a network of stories and autobiographies based on the combinations of different fragments, giving the impression you are immersing yourself in a fictional and literary world any time the (remote) opportunity to go online presents itself. It is an extremely varied world with its own set of rules, based on a sense of reciprocal co-belonging. Each user, with multiple interests and passions, participates in its multiple outputs, thus developing multi-dimensional identities. Thanks to the digital archaeology carried out by Internet Archive and Wayback Machine, I recently rediscovered some content from Splunge, which was closed by its owner around the same time (a fact that is entirely coincidental) that Facebook was growing in popularity in Italy, between 2007 and 2008. Among the finds, two seemed significant when read after the fact, as proof of continuity with what would follow.

The first is a post-dated 25 December 2006, in which Splunge reports the death of James Brown. The words used are the following: 'Tonight, on Christmas night, at 01:45 Atlanta time, James Brown died. Many, myself included, would be lying if we said we owned his albums or knew him as an artist, but it would be equally untrue to deny being moved upon hearing *Get Up I Feel Like Being a Sex Machine* or *I Got You (I Feel Good)* or that devilish riff from *Papa's Got a Brand New Bag* ... Keep staying on the scene (get on up!), and Merry Christmas.' In the blog post's well-populated comment section we find 'R.I.P.' written by the blog's participants, personal anecdotes on the influence of James Brown's music and links to other blogs containing similar reflections to those found on Splunge. From this we can deduce that today's social commemoration of dead celebrities, a subject of research in the inter-disciplinary field of Digital Death, had already been widespread in those contexts where interaction was virtual. The absence of YouTube means the commemoration is centred around written descriptions and images rather than videos. Furthermore, the lack of a single meeting place, as is the case with Facebook or Twitter, means that this commemoration is more dispersive and less available than it is today.

The second post, dated 24 March 2006, is entitled 'Shit Happens' and deals with the subject of digital oblivion. A technical error had led to numerous posts being deleted.

Splunge, while it notifies its readers that it is working on recovering the material through the RSS feeds saved on the host server and Google caches, reflects upon the volatile nature of online documents. Having expressed doubt about a complete recovery of all the lost texts, Splunge adds a significant postscript featuring the looped repetition of the warning: 'Remember to back up your files!' All this while never imagining that within a few years the blog would disappear in its entirety, along with most of the online spaces visited during the 1990s and the early 2000s, save a few fragments exhumed by Internet Archive.

As well as Splunge, I used a virtual hangout on MSN Messenger, born on 22 July 1999 as a simple message client, which became another world that ran parallel to the offline one, anticipating a number of social networks' basic prerogatives. MSN Messenger made it possible to personalize the background of your virtual habitat, to share images and GIFs (my personal favourite being Jason Newsted, Metallica's former bassist, doing the sign of the horns as an identificatory sign of heavy metal culture), and to bring your conversations to life with emoticons. Most importantly, it allowed you to write posts composed mostly of lines from favourite songs, without YouTube videos or the descriptions of emotional states accompanied by the usual dig 'you know who you are'. The anxiety provoked by a late or non-existent reply is not the sole prerogative of WhatsApp and its blue ticks: the *real time* aimed at by MSN Messenger anticipated the misunderstandings that have become a daily occurrence with the spread of instant messaging on mobile devices. For the first time ever, the user could appear either on or offline, and hold multiple conversations at the same time with both friends and strangers.

Back then, I would chat with my contacts on mailing lists created using multiple email inboxes. My brief foray into music journalism for two magazines dedicated to heavy metal and hard rock (one in print and one online) is entirely archived in two of these mailing lists, among hundreds of files containing reviews and live reports, requests for press accreditation at concerts, discussions on the layout of the next month's edition, and links to sites that are no longer used today. Despite using email, communication with other journalists did not necessarily occur with openly displayed names and surnames. Nicknames were even used in these contexts, meaning it was common to speak for years with people whose identities were entirely unknown to you. It is interesting to note that, despite having started to use email in 2000, the first sign of any actual email use dates from 3 October 2006. The previous six years disappeared into the ether the moment I downloaded my emails (alongside everyone else) from the server to Microsoft Outlook, which died alongside the computer I used at the time, lacking as I did the technical ability to resurrect it. A third mailing list for another online music magazine has also entirely disappeared. I can no longer remember the web portal on which I opened the specific email address, nor the access details. The magazine, called MusicbOOm, was closed several years ago. I may as well have imagined the entire thing.

A final online space in which I collected personal digital footprints in the pre-Facebook era was the forum on Kronic, a website dedicated to rock music. Again, years and years of anonymous conversations (as the participants were hiding their real identities behind the usual nicknames) have vanished completely, along with shared personal digital footprints. The only remaining fragments of Kronic can be found on Internet Archive, much like Splunge.

Facebook's origins are a kind of collage of all these previous experiences, which lay the foundations for the gradual creation of the definitive online version of the Library imagined by De Maria four decades earlier. Zuckerberg essentially extrapolates the main strong points from every previous invention, fashioning them into a single entity and amplifying their communicative potential by capitalizing on parallel digital revolutions that occur over the years. Working in favour of Facebook's progressive development are, more than anything else, the birth and development over the first decade of the twentieth century of mobile devices and YouTube, inaugurated 23 April 2005 at 20:27 with a nineteen-second video on the trunks of the elephants at San Diego zoo, which currently stands at seventy million views. The opportunity to enter the online dimension no matter where you are, no longer restrained by the time you might be able to set aside for sitting in front of a computer, along with YouTube's slogan, 'Broadcast Yourself', clear the way for a process of real mediatization, a gradual and decisive integration of the offline and online worlds, kept apart until now, which allows for the diffusion of social networks among generations. According to ComScore, in August 2008 some three months after its Italian version had been made available, Facebook registered almost eleven million users, with a 2,700% increase in subscribers in just one year.[27]

Mobile communication begins to favour the process of anthropological mutation theorized and so desired by advocates of the posthuman condition. And so, our doubles – the avatars or nicknames of the past – begin to integrate with the biological I in the management of our daily lives. Those using social networks in particular slowly grow accustomed to managing their own perspective in a fully operational way. Within an interactive graphic application, each user gains confidence with the possibility of altering the relationship they have with their visual surroundings. As Bolter and Grusin observe,

> She can remain in one place and move her viewing angle up and down, left or right, or side to side, in each case changing her perspective without changing her location relative to the objects that she sees. She can also keep her viewing angle fixed and move her point of view in three spatial dimensions: up or down, left or right, forward or back. [...]. What makes interactive computer graphics unique is that the shifts can now take place at the viewer's will.[28]

And this, as we will see, is one of the many elements that has determined the current metamorphosis of social networks into digital archives.

The Era of Shared Passions: An Epidemic of Digital Memories

In a passage from W.G. Sebald's novel *Austerlitz*, the narrator meditates gloomily on how little human beings are able to maintain of themselves. It seems that 'the world is, as it were, draining itself, in that the history of countless places and objects which themselves have no power of memory is never heard, never described or passed on'.[29] Sebald has a specific situation in mind: the progressive amnesia involving the places where the Nazi horrors were carried out. But his discourse could be extended to any physical object or place rendered obsolete by the passing of time and generations.

Conversely, today's world, just fifteen years on from the invention of Facebook and the dispersion of our personal digital footprints throughout the online world we have just described, is so suffocated by the accumulation and conservation of memories that we might ask ourselves whether we still have the capacity to forget. Rather than transforming us into consumers of a digital cocaine, social networks have turned us into 'ravenous consumerist zombies' intent on updating data flows 'the way zombies crave flesh'.[30] I will attempt to compile an inventory of all the data and digital information that occupies the spaces in which these zombies move today.

Facebook. According to data cited by Adam Ostrow, former editor-in-chief at *Mashable*, the average Facebook user shares around ninety documents a month on their own account. This means that, if they have signed up to Zuckerberg's social network, they have a personal account clearly indicating their name and surname and containing more than ten thousand documents including written reflections, photographs, GIFs, videos, stories and thousands of links to any number of political, cultural, social issues that have caught their attention over the years. Deaths, marriages, graduations, successes and failures are all collected and thrown together. To these we add the documents in which they have been tagged by their contacts over time, as well as the various footprints they have left both in other people's accounts and the public pages and groups on specific issues that interest them.

In other words, the average Facebook user, active since 2008, has filled their memory in just over ten years with tens of thousands of digital footprints from their existence. This refers to content that has *solely* been accrued on Facebook and does not include those marks left on other social networks and various other online spaces. This means that they can, at any moment of the day, recall in minute detail any personal, work, sentimental, family and any other event from the last ten years that has been registered and documented in their profile. In just a few minutes they can see the changes in their own personality, re-read their published posts, rediscover arguments with their contacts, look over photographs depicting them with people who are no longer in their lives, and so on. Bearing in mind that there are currently two billion Facebook users, each of them has the opportunity to use their computer or smartphone to consult billions of personal memories involving friends, family members, acquaintances, contacts never met offline and users who, despite not being a part of their circle of friends, have chosen to make their account public. Every time they leave the house, each one of these people will, with every probability, encounter individuals whom they have never met in person but about whose life stories they know key features, and whose personality they can outline in some detail. Just as happens in the Library imagined by De Maria in 1977. The habit of following the work, family and senti-mental intrigue of strangers is widespread: people with whom we would never enter into an offline relationship but who, for some reason or another, catch our attention as if they were characters in our favourite Netflix series.

A similar situation can be seen in the first social networks from the 1990s, in the period just before Facebook was born, albeit one with clear limits as the production and sharing of digital photographs was sporadic and video recordings were almost entirely absent. The weight of this material was not compatible with the kind of connection used to access the internet. Blogs and forums promoted written communication between people hidden behind nicknames, and this kind of communication, centred in particular on fantasy stories or exchanges of opinion on a specific topic, was entirely indif-ferent to personal life stories. Today, anyone using Facebook could, in theory, download the summer holiday photo albums shared over the last decade by two billion people. We pay little attention to this aspect but it is the clearest example of how our way of relating to private experiences has changed. Psychologist Giuseppe Riva describes today's online social networks as the creators of 'a hybrid social space' aimed at knowingly eliminating the barriers that once separated the various social networks to which each individual has always belonged.[31]

Twitter, Instagram, LinkedIn. The average Facebook user tends not to use just one social network. With all probability they also have a personal account on Twitter, with their tweets belonging to the 511,200 shared every minute throughout the world, and on Instagram, with their 'Stories' (a function that has become the communicative tool par excellence) adding to the 277,777 shared every 60 seconds. The time required to publish more than 55,000 photographs on the same network. For work they use LinkedIn, where everything they share on other social networks is usually joined by thousands of new documents that are, more often than not, of a professional nature.

YouTube. In their free time they might have opened an account on YouTube where, in a single minute, uploaded videos are viewed by almost five million people, each of whom could, in theory, download and share them again anywhere online. The opening episode of the television series *Black Mirror, The National Anthem* (2011), bases its implicit provocation on the viral nature of YouTube content. In this episode, the ransom set to ensure the safe release of the kidnapped princess demands the prime minister have sex with a pig live on national TV for all to watch. The video requesting the ransom is uploaded onto this platform by the kidnappers, viewed, downloaded and shared by hundreds of thousands of inter-connected citizens in just nine minutes.

In order to understand the lightning speed of YouTube's evolution from 2005 to today, helped in no small part by the parallel development of mobile devices and WiFi, let's pretend that this platform is used exclusively to find audio-visual material relating to Metallica concerts accumulated over the last twenty years or so. Official recordings and those taken from television appearances aside, the number of amateur videos from 1999 is scarce and limited to those few spectators who secretly smuggled their cumbersome video equipment into the concert venues. The recordings are erratic and the sound is muffled. There are far more amateur videos of Metallica concerts uploaded to YouTube in 2009, though still a comparatively low number. Here, however, we can spot among the hundreds of thousands of fans gathered in stadiums all over the world, dozens of cell phones attempting to record part of the show, unlike the shows from 1999 in which the public had no illuminated screens. But the number of phones is still limited with regard to the total number of audience members. However, an amateur video shared on YouTube in 2010 by the Italian comedy band *Elio e Le Storie Tese* is very telling. In it, during the obligatory ballad, the singer invites the public to raise not their traditional lighters but the illuminated screens of their cell phones. This brings us to the amateur videos of Metallica concerts uploaded to YouTube in 2019, which are literally innumerable. The expanse of illuminated smartphones in the audience is a truly awesome sight, and directly proportional to the vast number of videos documenting the American band's live performances on YouTube. Hundreds, if not thousands of official and amateur recordings of either single songs or entire concerts from all over the world are joined by videos of the most unusual, exciting or memorable moments from the show. In other words, in just twenty years, the way in which people record and conserve both public and private events has changed radically.

In 2019, in just one month, YouTube generated more content than the biggest film studios over the last sixty years. At the helm of the revolution in memory we are currently undergoing, YouTube is visited each month by more than a billion users and increases its audio and video material by 300 hours every minute. According to Simon Reynolds, it would take over two thousand years to watch all the platform's content, proving that we are not dealing with either a simple website nor mere technology. A symbolic demonstration of the 'astronomic expansion of humanity's resources of memory',[32] YouTube is a world composed of images and information hailing from every historical era and belonging to multiple forms of culture, constantly fragmented and broken down so they can be shared in perennially diverse modes and formats. Fontcuberta concludes that 'For the first time we are both the producers and the consumers of images, and the simultaneous accumulation of these has provoked an iconic, perhaps infinite landslide. The image is no longer a way of mediating the world, but an amalgam of it, if not its prime material.'[33]

Tumblr, Flickr. Fontcuberta's observation is confirmed by those social networks dedicated exclusively to photographic images. As well as Instagram, it is possible to have an account on Tumblr, in which almost one hundred thousand new images are uploaded every minute, and on Flickr, where twenty million images are viewed every sixty seconds. The sheer quantity of images present on Flickr has inspired two contemporary artworks.

The first is the project *Suns from Sunsets from Flickr*, which began in 2006 when artist Penelope Umbrico, wanting to photograph a romantic sunset, discovered that more than 540,000 images of romantic sunsets are archived on Flickr using the hashtag #sunset. The project, which is ongoing, brings together all of these images and creates a sort of mural covering the walls of a museum, with the composition updated gradually over the years. In 2016, ten years after the project began, Umbrico had over thirty million photographs of romantic sunsets on Flickr. Her ultimate aim was to confront those visiting her project with just how useless it was to continue photographing and sharing online images of a romantic sunset, as no matter the different places in which this particular subject is immortalized, all sunsets ultimately look the same.

The second work is the installation entitled *Photography in Abundance*, by Erik Kessels. First presented at the FOAM museum in Amsterdam at the end of 2011, the installation consists of pouring one and a half million photographs onto the ground, the same number of photographic images as are uploaded to Flickr in a single day. Downloaded from the internet and printed in the format of a traditional postcard, they are spread throughout several rooms in the building. According to Fontcuberta, if we dedicated just one second to each photograph, it would take two weeks to look at them all. In this way, visitors to the museum, especially those who have grown up in the era of analogue photography, can 'experience the stifling immersion in an ocean of images as if dragged by an unstoppable current. Rather than marvel, the audience feels overwhelmed and has the sensation they are drowning.'[34]

Academia.edu, Setlist.fm, Discogs, etc. The average Facebook user does not settle for the social networks mentioned this far. If you teach and carry out research in a university setting it is almost obligatory to have a personal profile on Academia.edu, a portal that allows you to share your publications with an international community made up of seventy million scholars. In other words, on Academia.edu we can find hundreds of millions of essays on any possible subject of university research that can be selected using the appropriate hashtags and downloaded for free in PDF format. In theory, anyone using this platform could potentially create a personal digital library on their own computer whose contents could number more than all of the hard copy content found in a national library.

If they are a music fan, they will undoubtedly have a personal profile on Setlist.fm, which has collated all the set lists of all the concerts by all the bands in the world from the 1970s onwards and is updated in real time during each concert. Furthermore, every user can create a setlist archive within their personal profile, listing all the concerts they have been to, particularly those featuring their favourite genres. They will then have a personal profile on Discogs, where they will build a digital archive of their own music library, sharing it with other users and actually creating a kind of digital swap shop. When discussing music, we must not forget Spotify, which allows the user to stream a selection of songs on demand (fourteen are uploaded every second) and produce their own playlists, which can also be shared with other users.

Private Messaging Apps and Email. As well as using social networks, we all primarily communicate with people we know using WhatsApp, Telegram and Messenger, sharing both new data (words, voice messages, photographs, videos) and data that has already been published on social networks. Hundreds, if not thousands or tens of thousands of conversations in which content that has accumulated over the years creates an epistolary whose breadth is historically unprecedented and can be consulted instantly. An epistolary enriched with missed calls, unanswered messages, and a significant quantity of phone numbers that can no longer be identified.

Personal communication then continues with email addresses, which contain the user's entire work and personal life from the late 1990s to date: lengthy exchanges, tickets from journeys made and shows attended, hotel bookings, banking transactions, dozens of login details from all kinds of websites (from supermarkets to libraries, dating sites and search engines such as Amazon), not to mention various personal documents (national insurance/ social security numbers, bank and credit card details, telephone numbers, and so on).

It is impossible to make an exhaustive inventory of all the places online where the user registers, shares and preserves traces of their existence in collaboration with others. Just think that every minute of the day some four and a half million searches are typed into Google, producing a total of six and a half billion a day.[35] In 2017, Kevin Kelly stated that 'every 12 months we produce 8 million new songs, 2 million new books, 16,000 new films, 30 billion blog posts, 182 billion tweets, 400,000 new products. With little effort today, hardly more than a flick of the wrist, an average person can summon the Library of Everything.'[36] Kelly added that even 'the total number of web pages, including those that are dynamically created upon request, exceeds 60 trillion. That's almost 10,000 pages per person alive. And this entire cornucopia has been created in less than 8,000 days.'[37]

From sex to food, from music to cinema, from reading to football, from politics to every form of social extravagance or peculiarity, there is no activity, situation or passion that has not been represented and recorded online using words and images, determining the continual and unstoppable birth of new online communities and new representations of the self. Luciano Floridi, citing a study by the UC Berkeley School of Information, compares the 12 exabytes of data accumulated by humanity over the course of history up to the widespread use of computers, with the 180 exabytes of data accumulated from that point until just 2006. Since then, data accumulation has grown so much that it has surpassed the zettabyte threshold (equivalent to 1000 exabytes). Floridi points out that, 'Every day, enough new data are being generated to fill all US libraries eight times over.'[38] The continual growth in data that goes hand in hand with the evolution of the technological devices available has led us into the 'Zettabyte Era', which represents a real 'tsunami of bytes that is submerging our environment'. This 'tsunami of bytes' leads Yuval Noah Harari to define today's era as one that has replaced faith in God with faith in data. Dataism is, therefore, the religion that believes the universe is constructed by a stream of data in such a way that the value of every phenomenon is determined by its contribution to data creation.[39]

Digital Memory as Crazed Mayonnaise: The Past is Emancipated, Identities Multiply

The current era of shared passions is bringing about far more radical anthropological, cultural, social, and political change compared to the time when precious access to the online world depended on two conditions being met: more free time and less exorbitant phone costs. Any understanding of digital technologies that still insists on a rigid separation and differentiation between the real and the virtual, the offline and online worlds, is decidedly obsolete. The previous paragraph proves how the metamorphosis of social networks into treasure chests of memories or digital archives, a metamorphosis that has taken just fifteen years, implies the online dimension increasingly resembles an entity that lacks its own specific territory, one that is dislocated by definition. Its numerous manifestations wilfully ignore our spatial-temporal habits offline, which occupy specific places at particular times. The absence of any specific territory and that total dislocation give rise to the surrealist vision of a dream culture, as maintained by Kenneth Goldsmith: 'We are awash in a new electronic collective unconscious [...] We speak on the phone while surfing the web, partially hearing what's being said to us while simultaneously answering e-mails and checking status updates.'[40]

The surrealist vision of a dream culture that makes this dislocation its central premise is destined to call into question every certainty regarding the concept of subjective identity that has been developed this far. Beyond the diverse interpretations provided by philosophy, anthropology and sociology over the course of history, the common denominator in subjective identity has always been equality and connection with the self, starting from the proof that no identity can *physically* occupy more than one place in the world. Though aware that different times, places and events can impose even the most radical transformations upon subjective identity – generally due to the inescapable role of inter-subjective context and the alternation between memory and forgetting – we rarely doubt the integrity of that identity. In today's world, the fusion of the online and offline dimensions into an 'onlife' reality causes the subjective identity to undergo a process of multiplication into various digital identities, making us 'informational organisms (*inforgs*), mutually connected and embedded in an informational environment (the infosphere)' shared alongside 'other informational agents, both natural and artificial, that also process information logically and autonomously'.[41] This situation leads to informational organisms becoming the protagonists of a post-individual and multi-identitarian mutation of the human being, in which every single human specimen becomes a collection of fragments that make up an interconnected global mind. In other words, each individual has become an 'algorithmic person' whose existence consists of the 'distribution of data, patterns, and interactions scattered across many platforms and interfaces'.[42]

Such data, structures and interactions, through the constant processes of dismantling and reconstruction we impose on our presence in the world, are slowly outlining the 'future trajectory' of an 'intimate engineering' that will lead to a lucrative convergence of algorithms and our desires for self-realization. Our subjective identity has multiplied to the point that its copies (as we will see) can take on an autonomous, independent life while continuing to represent the person who produced them. Today, this aspect, which will increasingly expand as technology evolves, already entails a radical distinction (at times, ontological) between hyper-connected human beings and those who either choose or are forced to live in the offline dimension only.

Dislocation and lack of a specific territory, the surrealist vision of a dreamlike culture, an inter-connected global mind: if these transformations that run parallel to the social networks' transformation into a digital memory chest call into question the certainties of those who were the first to experience the doubling of the world during the 1990s, they also entrust to the new generations the task of harnessing their consequences in the most lucrative way possible. Moritz Zimmermann, the seventeen-year-old nerd and protagonist of *How to Sell Drugs Online (Fast)*, a provocative German television series produced by Netflix, eloquently states the following at the beginning of the first episode: anyone belonging to generation Z, born between 1997 and 2012, has in their pocket, at this precise historical moment, the sum of human knowledge. They can become famous with one click and change the world without leaving their bed. Moritz, for example, follows his love rival's daily routines by simply monitoring what he shares on Instagram and Facebook, from which Moritz gleans all the necessary details with which to put together a character profile featuring all his habits and contradictions, and uses it to anticipate his moves.

There are other advantages, undoubtedly superior to those obtained by Moritz. For example, on a purely cultural level, the song *Old Town Road* by Lil Nas X (an artist from Atlanta born in 1999) set an unprecedented record thanks solely to his careful use of the internet. The song stayed at the top of the US Billboard Hot 100 for seventeen consecutive weeks, despite being released on an underground record label. The reason for its success lies in it going viral on TikTok, an application for mobile devices used by five hundred million adolescents and young people, in which users attempt to dub songs, miming or singing along with the original in the background. Lil Nas X's popularity on TikTok, where music is mixed with users' autobiographies, gave *Old Town Road* access to YouTube, using a video made exclusively for the web, and Spotify, where repeated plays have secured its success. In other words, the most popular song ever in the history of the United States was born, raised and developed exclusively online, and also found success in the offline dimension.

A good example of the complete fusion between online and offline in an onlife reality is SKAM, an intelligent Norwegian television series for teenagers that revolves around the use of social networks. Every episode, in which specific places, days and times are clearly indicated, shows the series' protagonists in both the offline and online dimensions. They go about their daily lives, each with a personal profile on Instagram and Facebook on which they post messages, images and videos over the course of the episode. What is innovative about SKAM is that the plot also develops in brief daily clips, published online in real time and integrated with the social profiles that have genuinely been created by the actors starring in SKAM. This ensures that each day audience members can observe the lives of their darlings in real time by connecting to the site that collates the daily clips and their social profiles. SKAM also has its own Spotify playlist, which is obviously updated as the story progresses. All of this material, subdivided into clips and posts on social profiles, makes up the entirety of the next week's episode.

The new reality we are now living in proves that the decision taken by Desmond Morris to erase all material traces of his dead wife in order to limit the pain caused by her absence, is impossible for anyone immersed in the onlife world. Anyone actively using the web can no longer think of the past as a story told only to ourselves or as a simulation of the mind. What happens, then, to our memory and the alternation between memory and forgetting? In his review of my previous book, Francesco Paolo de Ceglia uses an expression as amusing as it is effective: 'the informational soul holds on to everything, albeit in a disorganized way, like crazed mayonnaise'.[43] Each one of us endlessly shares and registers our own digital footprints as if they were crazed mayonnaise. All actions in the online world lack a unifying thread to bring coherence to the whole; they are purposefully fragmentary and proud of their sloppiness. We introduce ourselves with our name and surname in every social network we use, but we could, in theory, open other accounts perhaps illegally under false names, using the material shared by other users with public privacy settings, appropriating the identities of others. We could continue using nicknames and pseudonyms like we did in the 1990s, in any other online community or setting we frequent. We could correspond for years with strangers we have never met in real life, but whose life story we know more intimately than their own relatives. It is digital transformism: we can create new collective identities that change from one minute to the next, chaotically intersecting with one another, amplifying and problematizing the themes surrounding social memory in today's world.

The crazed mayonnaise our memory hides behind generates unprecedented situations that are not theoretically predictable. For example, I have played SongPop on Facebook since 2011, an online game in which the aim is to guess the song title in the shortest time possible, with multiple challenges against other players. The game also allows you to communicate with those other players using private messages. In this way I have message threads (some serious, some less so) dating back almost ten years with people I interact with almost daily on Songpop, and whom I therefore frequent more than some friends or acquaintances. What importance will this collection of communicative traces be given when it comes to a future reconstruction of my memories?

Another example are birthdays. Until a few years ago, everyone received a finite number of birthday wishes via a phone call or greetings card. Creating your own archive of greetings cards was a simple and immediate operation. Today, anyone using a number of social networks will receive hundreds of birthday wishes from people they do and do not know, to which we can add the written and voice messages on WhatsApp, Messenger and Telegram. Sometimes even on LinkedIn. As well as having to spend a significant amount of time responding to all of the messages, creating an archive of them becomes impossible.

There are numerous ways in which we manage our own digital memories, to the point that it becomes impossible (as we have seen) to create a complete inventory of our own shared memories. Think of the long, polemical correspondence between the two philosophers Fichte and Schelling, who argued ferociously over their different ways of understanding the concept of nature. If they had lived today, these disagreements would take place over posts shared reciprocally on Facebook, perhaps also in the captions underneath photographs on Instagram and (why not?) privately using email, WhatsApp voice messages or private message on Messenger. Who can be sure that they wouldn't argue on dozens of YouTube videos, with a fixed camera filming them sitting in their home libraries? It would certainly be impossible to perfectly reconstruct the outlines of their arguments, as they would be dispersed over various online locations. Now, we could rightly observe that the physical archives containing the letters of one of the two philosophers would be entirely destroyed if, for example, there were a fire. Digital archives, though dispersive, do not run this same risk as they can be duplicated ad infinitum and/or are present online. However, unlike physical archives, digital archives must reckon with the problem of technological obsolescence, of formats and hard drives, the effect of which isn't that dissimilar to that of fire on a physical archive.

James Bridle, in a decidedly apocalyptic tone, connects the inability to manage this crazed mayonnaise of data with the belief that the current era is a 'new dark age':

> And so we find ourselves today connected to vast repositories of knowledge, and yet we have not learned to think. In fact, the opposite is true: that which was intended to enlighten the world in practice darkens it. The abundance of information and the plurality of worldviews now accessible to us through the internet are not producing a coherent consensus reality, but one riven by fundamentalist insistence on simplistic narratives, conspiracy theories, and post-factual politics. It is on this contradiction that the idea of a new dark age turns: an age in which the value we have placed upon knowledge is destroyed by the abundance of that profitable commodity, and in which we look about ourselves in search of new ways to understand the world.[44]

Douglas Rushkoff, on the other hand, sees not so much a new dark age as a kind of 'digital unconscious', as from the moment data are recorded in the online dimension it becomes simultaneously both present and absent. Everything is recorded, almost nothing is accessible, and all it takes is a change in the file's format or a programme update to suddenly make information that had, up until that moment, been easily accessible, useless.[45]

Crazed mayonnaise, new dark age, digital unconscious: no matter how we define the current technological era and digital memory, we must attempt to analyse the changes to how we remember and forget, starting with an under-standing of the narrative peculiarities of social networks and the internet in general. As we will see over the next chapter, social networks seem, on the one hand, to be experiments in collective cultural autobiography, but, on the other, they appear as encyclopedias of the dead version 2.0. The fact they can assimilate to both narrative solutions, despite not wholly identifying with either, will lead to a careful analysis of the specific temporal dialectic that is developed within them in contrast to the one that characterizes the offline world. The biggest problem in holding the 'real' and the 'virtual' together in an onlife reality comes precisely from the different temporalities that sets them apart.

2

Collective Cultural Autobiographies and Encyclopedias of the Dead 2.0

Experiments in Collective Cultural Autobiography

In his book *Wasting Time on the Internet*, Kenneth Goldsmith defines Facebook as 'a grand experiment in collective cultural autobiography'.[1] In just fifteen years more than two billion people have gathered within a shared inter-subjective and interactive environment that puts them each in a position where they update their own biographical profile day in, day out. Through the daily use of words and images that are recorded and preserved, every user tells both their past experiences and those happening in real time. They are also given the opportunity to gain insight into the personal profiles belonging to others. As Tomás Maldonado observes, there is no autobiographical memory, either narrated or written, that is entirely autonomous and in no way influenced or conditioned by those who are listening or reading: 'the presence of others contributes to the modification, sometimes substantial, of the nature of our tale'.[2] To narrate is to remember: every episode of our own life that is narrated, from the most profound to the most insignificant, it anticipates a relationship of reciprocal involvement between the narrator and those listening; so the link between the individual's ongoing autobiographical memory and their interpersonal relationships, and the way in which they are articulated in space and time, is inextricable. This is obviously overwhelmingly valid in an interactive and public environment such as Facebook, where 'the others' do not limit themselves to simply listening, reading and (if called for) providing some suggestion or advice, but actively intervene using written words, photographic images and audio-visual recordings. The guiding principle of social networks is the following: there is no personal expression that does not determine the simultaneous involvement of others. As such, every shared and recorded text is joined by the opinions of other people, which cooperate in order to extend and amplify that text, rendering it more complex (or, conversely, more banal), even when the discussion is invalidated by trolls or haters, causing it to degenerate into self-serving arguments or insults. Take, for example, a simple post in which a single user expresses a personal opinion on a particular argument. In the comments, this issue is discussed and expanded to such an extent that (at times) the initial post is modified several times over by observations made by others, regardless of whether they are pertinent or incoherent.

Furthermore, Facebook allows each of its users to bear witness to the most significant events taking place in the society they belong to through the sharing and collective discussions of articles from national and international journalism alongside cultural, artistic, social and political events, generating a public reflection on that which has marked both the era ushered in by the birth of Zuckerberg's creature and the years that preceded it.

To sum up: the grand experiment in collective cultural autobiography, as Goldsmith refers to Facebook, consists of two billion people benefiting from the possibility of publicly shaping their own biography and that of others, while at the same time narrating historic events that, day after day, define the social, cultural and political memory of recent years. Autobiographical memory and collective memory tend, therefore, to meld together, creating a synthesis between the memory of personal events and the collection of signs and symbolic practices with which the memory of a group is constituted on the screens of their computers and smartphones on a daily basis.

Future historians will likely have the detailed representation of an entire civilization during a specific era at their disposal thanks to this cooperation unburdened by spatial limits, which, generated through a daily use of the internet, has been amplified by social networks. For example, if social predictions made in 2019 with regard to the probable end of the world in 2050 due to environmental calamity and global warming are not correct (*ça va sans dire*), they will no doubt find them highly entertaining. At the same time, they will despair about the way in which the users commented on those predictions and discussed them. We should never forget that within social networks we find the same sentiments that De Maria attributed to those visiting his imaginary Library in 1977: 'cries of fury and pain in relentless successions, fragments of sentences and pleas addressed to God-knows-who'.[3]

In order to delve further into how Facebook may resemble an experiment of collective cultural autobiography, I think it would be useful to use two different examples, both of which demonstrate a connection between individual experiences and the flow of data in general, which points to the structural complexity of the narrative context found in social networks, not to mention the particular dynamics to which the dialectic between remembering and forgetting is subject.

The first example involves the sharing on my personal wall, on 25 February 2018, of a photograph of the official ticket for Nirvana's concert in Milan on the same day in 1994. To be clear, this is the same photograph referred to in the book's introduction in the description of Facebook's Memories section. Sharing this photo was testament, first and foremost, to a specific event in my life: attending an alternative rock concert during a particular time in my life – adolescence. Secondly, it evokes many details of the event – the atmosphere in the crowd, the name of the opening act (the Melvins), the setlist followed by Kurt Cobain and friends, the weather, etc. – thanks to the dialogical exchange that takes place beneath the shared image twenty-five years later between fans of the Seattle band who also follow me. Thirdly, it documents a series of secondary information that may nevertheless reveal itself to be fundamental in an historical reconstruction of customs at that time: the cost in Italian lire of a concert by one of the most popular bands of the early 1990s (32,000 lire), the approximate capacity of the venue (ascertained through the entrance number printed on the ticket: 8,211), a collection of clues as to the way concerts were organized at that time (the design of the ticket, the kind of venue, the rules for attendance, and so on). Finally, it implicitly superimposes two different moments in time – 25 February 1994 and the same day in 2018 – to which many others can be added. All I would need to do is reshare the image of the ticket at any point in the future, perhaps prompted once more by the Memories section, thus activating a new discussion among my contacts that makes the original sharing of the photo current and brand new for the umpteenth time.

The second example instead involves a recent Italian news story. The national newspapers report the news of the disappearance of Elisa and Massimo, two young people from the province of Piacenza. Elisa's Facebook account, whose publications had only ever been managed by her until the day of her death, became a digital meeting place, not just for friends and family but for everyone who, having read the news and searched online for the woman's digital identity, ended up there out of curiosity. Elisa's friends and sisters, making the most of the account's public privacy settings, began to publish photos that showed her in the most varied of settings. The accompanying captions contain a meticulous description of the various memories linked to past experiences they had shared. While the aim is to convince the woman to come out of hiding, its first consequence is to make a number of (for the most part) private memories public and easily accessible to anyone. These are then shared with the implicit agreement of the account holder, as the privacy settings set previously allowed this action. Gradually, as the police investigation develops, Elisa's profile is viewed by an ever-growing number of curious onlookers. Once the woman's murder (by Massimo) is exposed, the significance of the account suddenly alters. It goes from being a place of memory to a place of commemoration, where hundreds of people leave messages of condolence. The solemnity required by the circumstances is flanked by an unfortunate intrusiveness that verges, at times, on tragic comedy. The following exchange between two strangers demonstrates this very well:

- User X: *Now you are an angel in heaven.*
- User Y: *What do you know? She might've been an atheist.*

Not just an unusual location for digital farewells, Elisa's account also becomes an open space in which an improvised collective debate on femicide in Italy is developed, discussing the ways it is reported in the news and so on. As if that weren't enough, it is joined by thousands of tweets on Twitter and images on Instagram which, grouped together under a hashtag featuring the victim's name and surname, bring even more facts, information and details about her private life into the spotlight of public opinion.

Though very different, these two examples reveal important details regarding the way autobiographical narratives develop within social networks through continual juxtapositions.

Firstly, they demonstrate the inevitable lack of a unifying thread to (as is usually the case in traditional autobiographical works) provide coherence and linearity to the collection of different narratives in cooperation with others. They are chaotic pills of language, disarticulated offcuts of information, fleeting moments of representation, repeated reiterations of memories that are both different and the same. Facebook's very structure makes it impossible to create an ordered, exhaustive and definitive reconstruction of all the digital footprints a single user leaves within it. Indeed, not only does each user publish in the designated areas on their own account, but they are also able to write on those belonging to their contacts, on public pages, on subject groups and, if they so choose, even on the accounts of those who, despite not featuring among their personal contacts, have chosen to make their profile public. Just as happened in Elisa's case. It is impossible, therefore, to group together all of the words and images recorded by a Facebook user to create a kind of coherent inventory of their interactions, one that follows a rational order. To further complicate the narrative context are numerous variables that can be traced back to the multiple and fragmentary nature of digital identities. For example, deleting an account leads to the elimination (temporary or permanent) of everything the user has recorded on the social network. It follows that it is often possible to read posts shared years earlier in which, in the comments section, the dialogical exchange is reduced to a kind of written soliloquy, missing the words of those who have deleted their profiles. It is as if, in the offline world, the death of one's partner automatically eliminated their presence from personal memories of every conversation ever held. Similarly, each user can re-select memories from the past, which are inevitably modified each time, as we see in the case of the Nirvana ticket mentioned above. They can even delete them selectively, continually reshaping the social narrative of their lives and that created with other users as they see fit.

Secondly, the experiment in collective cultural autobiographical that Goldsmith identifies solely with Facebook must be extended to all those other social networks in regular use, as they are all closely bound. This provides us with a doubly effective way of understanding cultural autobiography in the online dimension.

If we view all social networks as connected, we can build a global autobiographical narrative that is unprecedented in history, comprising a colossal amount of schizophrenic words, images and videos. It is what accounts for the countless traces on our screens of a single interconnected global mind that 'acts as an invisible hand leading individuals to merge with the swarm'.[4]

If instead we consider each social network separately, we can see the different modalities used to articulate the autobiographical memory constructed by the individual in cooperation with other users. Facebook favours the written word, Twitter favours ultra-short texts known as Tweets that feature just 280 characters, while Instagram uses photographic images and TikTok and YouTube videos. The fact that each social network prefers a particular expressive modality does not, obviously, exclude any other. For example, adolescents compose their narratives (particularly on TikTok) by blending together videos that immortalize them dancing to songs that play in the background, and tales (that are generally sentimental, though truthful to varying degrees) created using concise written texts that are joined by the numerous comments made by other, equally concise users.

An interesting, not to mention bizarre, example of an autobiographical narrative different to that developed by Facebook, one using video recordings, is *mukbang* on YouTube. The result of the crasis in Korean between 'eat' and 'broadcast', *mukbang* indicates a collection of live-streamed videos in which single users record themselves as they eat, usually loudly and with an emphatically dramatic emphasis, while chatting to hundreds or thousands of online users in the comments section. The phenomenon, which began in South Korca in 2009, spread throughout the world and has become an (at times ridiculous) occasion in which an individual livestreams themselves eating a meal, on their own or in company, while recounting tales from their personal life linked to food and interactions with the other people participating in the virtual banquet, hidden behind their computer screens. The result is the serial recording of a remarkable number of videos that generate an autobiographical narrative developed around the specific subject of food. This narrative is both individual, if you only consider the number of videos made by a single person, and collective, if you add up all the videos connected through the hashtag #mukbang. Some people use this kind of narrative to deal with their own eating disorders (bulimia or anorexia, for instance), as food-voyeurism seems to extinguish any desire for food. Others have transformed it into an antidote to loneliness, because, as we experience on a daily basis in the onlife reality, eating alone but connected to many strangers is an alternative way to create the company lacking in the offline dimension. Some videos reach millions of views and feature hundreds of comments.

This phenomenon obviously has a dark side, typical of the multiplication of digital identities in a prevalently individualistic historical moment, such as the illusion that the community created between digital identities will entirely eliminate the potential loneliness of biological identity. As we will see in many more cases, the problem hidden within the concept of a human being as a multi-identitary entity is the total identification of its copies with the original psychophysical presence. The multiple digital identities represent an extension of, or in any case a brand-new opportunity for each individual, but not a substitution or alternative. As long as we recognize that they extend but do not substitute our existence, then the virtual banquet between numerous digital identities can be yet another opportunity to find company.

Copy and Paste: Writing About Oneself is Like Summing Up the History of the Universe

In his attempt for delve further into the extremely composite nature of this particular kind of narrative, Goldsmith's interpretation goes a step further. In his book *Uncreative Writing*, he demonstrates how the transformation of (for the most part, dispersive and decontextualized) fragments of words and images into a 'multimedia autobiographical text' is leading us to radically rethink the very concepts of writing and language, not to mention temporal rationality. The online proliferation of written texts, for example, means that these texts are constantly being remixed, calling into discussion any certainty regarding ownership, responsibility or memory:

> Words very well might not only be written to be read but rather to be shared, moved, and manipulated, sometimes by humans, more often by machines, providing us with an extraordinary opportunity to reconsider what writing is and to define new roles for the writer. While traditional notions of writing are primarily focused on 'originality' and 'creativity', the digital environment fosters new skill sets that include 'manipulation' and 'management' of the heaps of already existent and ever-increasing language.[5]

In other words, the communal nature of multimedia autobiographical texts found on social networks, in which artistic value is attributed to the concepts of the collective manipulation, remixing and organization of language, leads to uncreative writing: a collective way of writing that confers a qualitative primary role to plagiarism, theft, copy and paste, to the free appropriation of other people's texts, to widespread cooperation between multiple subjects involved in writing, and to literary solidarity.

Can I steal that? and I'm going to use that! are, respectively, the recurring question and imperative used by the user who, having read a post on a Friend's wall, wants to share it in turn with their followers on their own profile (perhaps embellishing it with a personal consideration). A somewhat unusual theft, in that permission is requested before it takes place, or, alternatively, publicly admitted once it has happened. This 'theft' is proof of how every text written and shared by a single user is both a specific expression of their singularity and one of an infinite number of fragments within a single interactive environment in which the one and the many are publicly melded together, in almost pantheistic terms, in order to define the general characteristics of the world and reality to which they belong. Collective action, not individual contemplation. According to Kevin Kelly, 'on the screen we assemble our myths from pieces. On networked screens everything is linked to everything else. The status of a new creation is determined not by the rating given to it by critics but by the degree to which it is linked to the rest of the world. A person, artefact, or fact does not "exist" until it is linked.'[6]

This peculiar form of collective multimedia autobiography brings to mind the words used by Schelling in the nineteenth century to introduce *The Ages of the World*: 'certainly one who could write completely the history of their own life would also have, in a small epitome, concurrently grasped the history of the cosmos'.[7]

The Ages of the World is an unfinished work that aimed to outline, over three books, the past, the present and the future of the entire world according to the philosophical, mythological and theosophical knowledge acquired over the years. Such an ambitious task pushes Schelling, ever faithful to the pantheistic imperatives inherent in nineteenth-century German romanticism, to identify philosophical thought with a truly autobiographical knowledge, and to define the human being as a microcosm. With the use of this term he highlights the correspondence between all processes of human life (from the unconscious to the fully conscious) and all processes of universal life. Every individual, much like the average social network user, develops a number of identities based on relationships, interaction and exchange, and these behave as if in a 'living rotation', a living circuit, placing themselves within a dense network of relationships that condition the way they exist in the world, with which they develop a reciprocal correspondence (an aspect that is anything but taken for granted in the philosophical era of idealistic subjectivism). The living circuit can only organize itself if it does not elude that which, from the outside, radically influences its way of doing so, modifying it according to particular problems and occasions. This organization, mediated by external determination, keeps track of a series of constants to which each of us is subjected. Life always begins in the dark, no one ever makes out the ultimate aim of everything, and a clear understanding of any single event extrapolated from its wider context is generally out of the question. In theory, one could grasp the entire course of events, but only once it has reached completion. Take history: we can, both in reality and fiction, gradually retrace the different stages that led to its development, but only if we know the final outcome in advance.

If the human is a microcosm with the qualities we have listed above, every single individual, precisely because they are an 'eternal article' of the world, holds within them the entirety of things that make them unique and their perspective, impossible to repeat.[8] The sum of the fragments in the world is equivalent to the sum of drops in the sea: both the world and the sea, in their totality, are respectively contained in every single fragment and every single drop of water. Each fragment and each drop, no matter how indistinguishable they may seem, are central to making the world and the sea what they are. There is, therefore, a reciprocal correspondence between the biographical history of every individual (despite them being single and unique) and the entire history of the universe. In an aphorism, published a few years before *Ages of the World* in 1806, Schelling delves deeper into this correspondence with a further poetic metaphor:

> Each soul knows the infinite; each soul knows everything but in an indeterminate way. Though one perceives the roaring of the forest during a storm, what is actually heard is the rustling of each leaf, but it is combined with that of every other and

cannot be distinguished. Such is the rumbling and tumult of the world of our soul.[9]

Social networks today seem to offer an online space designated for anyone who wishes to clarify and, above all, record the tumult and background noise of the world that exists within their own soul, using their own narratives and those of others. As they write and record their own life stories on social networks together with the other two billion people like them, each one of them sums up the entire history of the universe. This is possible precisely because of the uncreative writing discussed by Goldsmith. A form of writing that favours the connection to the single presence, emphasizing the multi-identitarian and post-individualistic character of the hyperconnected human being, as the TV series SKAM discussed earlier demonstrates so efficiently.

Cancer Bloggers: My Body is My Message

Many of those analysing the current digital revolution are profoundly sceptical when it comes to the opportunities for narrative and autobiography offered by social networks. Rather, they find objective proof, be it in phenomena such as *mukbang* or simple interactions on Facebook, that there is a radical (qualitative) difference between the offline and online dimensions. In other words, they insist on that dualistic understanding typical of the 1990s that rigidly distinguishes between the 'real' and the 'virtual', and that therefore ignores the changes that have occurred in recent years. In the continual breakdown of our singularity into millions of pieces of data, Byung-Chul Han, for example, perceives not so much a 'living circuit' of Schelling-esque memory, but a 'senseless void'.[10] He insists that, in online activity, the accumulation of personal digital footprints and marks never actually leads to an authentic knowledge or real awareness, or to qualitative extensions of our identity. In the same way, he insists that the interaction with one's own contacts within social networks is not a real encounter with the other: 'one lusts after adventures and stimulation, but always remains *the same*'.[11] All online representations, first and foremost selfies as 'the self in empty forms',[12] are nothing but *adipose emptiness of fullness* that merely disintegrate and atrophy all forms of supportive proximity.[13] Sherry Turkle maintains that digital culture leads to the destruction of the three chairs – one for solitude, two for friendship, three for society – that Henry David Thoreau kept in his cabin. Not connection but solitude. According to Turkle, communication within social networks impedes the development of healthy introspection and a constructive internal dialogue that, by teaching us to make peace with solitude, lays the foundations for our productive communication with others. Instead, by always using digital technology in order to socialize, we find ourselves living autistically within a falsely communitarian dimension, in which there is no difference between a conversation with another person via social media or a conversation with the various chatbots (Alexa and co.) at our disposal. Finally, Manfred Spitzer, in his text tellingly entitled *Connessi e isolate* [*Connected Yet Isolated*], confirms (using an impressive number of statistics) a drop in emotional participation in the activities of others from the moment in which communication via social media overtakes that maintained offline.[14]

Though very much worthy of our attention for the meticulous way in which they highlight a number of objective issues inherent in the daily use of social media, Han, Turkle and Spitzer tend to underestimate a number of beneficial effects both of the anthropological mutation taking place, which moves towards a total integration of the online and offline dimensions, and digital memory being understood as an increasingly social experience. Indeed, Han, connecting more or less explicitly the daily use of social networks and the elevation of productivity as the only form of life, maintains that the digital revolution is silencing death and subjecting illness to health hysteria. It is precisely this last consideration that allows us, however, to highlight how the creation of interactive autobiographical memories that favour connection to a single presence generates consequences that are anything but negative within the current bond between the use of digital technology and the collection of problems concerning death and illness.

Over the last three decades, this bond has been studied using two neologisms: *Thanatechnology* and *Thanatosensitivity*. The first, coined by sociologist Carla Sofka in 1997, indicates the various technological and digital mechanisms that allow us to access information on the deceased and that most importantly provide us with stories, commemorations and assorted multimedia expressions that help us confront the management and elaboration of illness and grief, as well as nurturing hope (often highly creative) for individual immortality. The second neologism, coined in 2009 by scholars Michael Massimi and Andrea Charise, describes the integration of mortality, dying and death within those systems in which there is an interaction between humans and computers. The two scholars define 'mortality' as the ontological condition of the human being: 'death' as a specific act or event that happens in a particular moment, acting as a watershed between before and after; and finally, 'dying' as the temporary phase of progressive decline in health that lies halfway between mortality and their death. *Thanatosensitivity*, involving disciplines from the humanities, technology and science, consists of an in-depth analysis of the transformations undergone by mortality, dying and death as a result of the progressive development of digital technologies. The constant mutation of the way in which we understand the dialectic between the real and the virtual in human life that has followed this development also has ethical consequences that are yet to be explored.[15]

Today, the evolution of these neologisms is closely linked to the ways in which online autobiographical memories and digital archives are used in the varied context of Digital Health, an inter-disciplinary field of research that aims to provide innovative tools to help both health operatives and individuals face the most painful moments in their lives.

One of the most interesting uses of online autobiographical memories is that by 'cancer bloggers'. This term tends to be used for individuals who, having been diagnosed with a tumour, decide to publish writing, photographic images and videos on social networks to *publicly* narrate their own health condition and the subjective fears to which this gives rise. Those who prefer to recount their illness using video open a personal channel on YouTube; those who instead prefer to use photographic images use their own

Instagram profiles; those who prefer written reflections turn to their Facebook accounts. In all three cases (though most tend to integrate all three), a narrative is created using words, photographs and videos through which the patient becomes a kind of *influencer* with a high number of followers, creating a network around themselves and their illness. If, as Goldsmith observes, language is becoming a material or substance 'that moves and morphs through its various states and digital and textual ecosystems',[16] it is particularly useful to use this mobility and metamorphosis that takes place in a digital context to invent brand new stories with which to break down the social and cultural taboos that make our everyday lives problematic.

The cancer bloggers' main objective is, in fact, to utilize the public sharing of their own illness in order to circumvent (1) any exclusion from the 'club of the living' that usually happens to the patient in their offline life once medical diagnosis objectively confirms the presence of a serious pathology; and (2) the following phase of marginalization that the patient must face while they are subjected to incapacitating oncological treatments.[17] As Dr Atul Gawande observes in his book *Being Mortal*, contemporary society still attributes a kind of moral blame to illness, which makes it very difficult to avoid the patient ending up in an isolation that makes their treatment even more problematic. 'We end up with institutions that address any number of societal goals – from freeing up hospital beds to taking burdens off families' hands to coping with poverty among the elderly – but never the goal that matters to the people who reside in them: how to make life worth living when we're weak and frail and can't fend for ourselves anymore.'[18]

This inability to provide comfort and attention to the terminally ill derives first and foremost (though not exclusively) from the fact that in the illness and death of others we see the very real possibility of the same happening to us and the certainty of our own death, a subject usually kept at a safe distance. In 1926 in her brief essay *On Being Ill*, Virginia Woolf was already explaining the marginal role of illness in literature with the deliberate choice by authors to regularly depict the body as 'a sheet of plain glass through which the soul looks straight and clear'.[19] The body must, therefore, keep at bay the carnal perishability that defines it. Virginia Woolf's thoughts find numerous philosophical equivalents, one of which is clearly expressed in the words used by Horkheimer and Adorno in their *Dialectic of Enlightenment.* According to the two philosophers, over the course of historical and theoretical development Western thought has never stopped *mechanizing* the body, limiting itself to conceiving the body as a simple organic equivalent to the watch and attributing it a less important role than that of the intellect.[20] An organism is *alive* because *it works*, because it fulfils its own functions by resisting illness and death; it is *dead* because *it doesn't work*, because its 'mechanisms' have not been able to fight the insurgent illness. The organism is therefore seen as a machine whose intrinsic value is enclosed in its performance capacity, its efficiency and its ability to maintain itself. The illness, understood as a malfunction that must necessarily be repaired, only emphasizes this negative conception to which corporeity is subjected, appearing as a kind of residual life, a leftover from production in which the execrable human fallibility is reflected. And as such, the death that follows represents the greatest social anomaly in existence as it cannot be planned for by the cumulative system that otherwise strives for perfection.

For cancer bloggers, the collection of multimedia autobiographical texts becomes a significant opportunity for sharing, as well as a tool for social and cultural emancipation. They assimilate their own psycho-physical presence with the (intangible) message that they communicate to and direct at others. A message which survives them precisely because it is immaterial. The absence of physicality, where the body is substituted by its online image, makes that which they communicate (through written and voice messages, photographs, videos) their digital body. They are, at the same time, both the subject and the object of the story. As such, the identification between the communicated message and the digital body disinhibits them and alleviates the embarrassment felt during a face-to-face encounter. This disinhibition ensured by the protection and distance offered by digital screens makes the story of the reality of one's own illness more explicitly immediate, integrating it into one's autobiography in the making as constructed on social networks, and allowing, in turn, for the 'normalization' of the patient's condition. The refuge within a secure network of those who have had or are having the same experience makes the tumour a painful biological eventuality that can materialize in every single organism and not, therefore, a moral fault that rigidly draws the line between the world of the healthy and that of the sick. The likes, comments and shares compensate, albeit partially, for the daily suffering. And ultimately, narrating one's own illness gives the impression of being useful to others, allowing them to tell a story in which the subject and the object live on forever, beyond death. Cancer bloggers demonstrate the positive impact of this priority of connection over individual contributions developed in autobiographical narratives on social networks.

Stories of Cancer Bloggers on YouTube and Facebook

There are two cases on YouTube that particularly struck me. One is that of Talia Joy Castellano, a young girl affected by a rare form of cancer from the age of seven that caused her death after six years of illness on 16 July 2013. During the final phase of the illness, Castellano became an internet star, opening her own YouTube channel in 2011 under the name 'TaliaJoy18'. Here she shared more than two hundred videos followed by tens of thousands of people. This channel, still active today, hosts a long series of make-up tutorials, a particular passion for the girl. The decision to make these tutorials came about when chemotherapy caused her to lose her hair. In one of her many videos, Talia defines make up as her wig. Many of the recordings on TaliaJoy18 deal with personal reflections on her physical condition, her various hospital stays and, obviously, the ensuing concerns. A guest on a number of television broadcasts and the object of various blogs set up exclusively in her honour, the girl has always spoken openly about her likely death, using a tautological expression in one of her last videos that immediately went viral as a kind of therapeutic meme: 'When it's my turn to go, that will be my turn to go.' A Wikipedia page on the girl was set up, and after her death, TaliaJoy18 became an archive of personal memories on YouTube with a double purpose: to keep her memory alive and to offer her experience as an aid to those facing the same ordeal.[21]

The second case is that of 33-year old Daniel Edward Thomas from England who, on 11 January 2018, opened the page PeeWeeToms on YouTube where he published an introductory video in which he reveals that he has a sarcomatoid carcinoma, a very aggressive form of cancer, and that he wants to talk about his daily life with the disease and chemotherapy. Nine months later, PeeWeeToms had more than 162,000 subscribers and had published just under two hundred videos. In some he recounts his experience with cancer and chemotherapy, his hopes and fears. Others feature rare moments of happiness, such as his wedding. In one of these videos, viewed by more than 200,000 people, Daniel says that talking about his tumour makes him feel free. In another, viewed by more than two million users, he reveals, in tears, the negative verdict given by the doctors regarding the possibility of his recovery. In the meantime, his parents create the page PeeWeeMoms & PaPaToms, in which they describe in meticulous detail the changes imposed on a life that has to deal with a child's cancer diagnosis. It is on this page that Daniel's parents inform their followers of his death, on 28 September 2018. His funeral, announced on YouTube, was attended by hundreds of people, many of whom only knew Daniel online thanks to his audio-visual accounts.

Among the many similar cases found on Facebook, worth a particular mention is the page 'Anime belle di Teresa Calvano' [The Beautiful Souls of Teresa Calvano] – #FuckCancer, managed up until the day she died by Teresa Calvano, a thirty-year old woman from Andria (Italy) who recounted her life marked by osteosarcoma from December 2015 to New Year's Eve 2018. She formed a community of almost twenty thousand people – the 'beautiful souls' – and maintained this group until the final moment of her life. She shared thoughts, videos, images in which she is always shown wearing very colourful scarves covering the signs of chemotherapy. She created the '(T)urbanwave', a series of coloured turbans for women perfect for use during chemotherapy, which she decided to donate to Italian oncology departments.

Anyone can contribute to this initiative through a one-off donation. In her final video, on New Year's Eve, she wishes her 'beautiful souls' a happy new year, mentioning that her health situation has become increasingly critical. She says, however, that make up and her colourful look keep her morale up. She concludes by stating that she is the happiest person in the world, followed by three hashtags: #Fuckosteosarcoma #hope #fanculo2018 (literally, #fuckoff2018). Within the first few days of 2019, a relative gave news of her death. They write that they have no intention of talking directly to Teresa, because they are conscious that someone who dies does not have access to a WiFi connection. They thank all of those who have shared her stories over the months. As with the TaliaJoy18 YouTube channel, Teresa Calvano's page is still active, both to keep the woman's daily accounts alive, which can be useful for those facing the same situation, and to continue her work. Her relatives have continued to produce and distribute colourful scarves, while fundraising for associations working to fight cancer. These activities are integrated in the offline dimension with evenings dedicated to Teresa's memory, during which psychologists and doctors discuss cancer, patients undergoing chemotherapy model colourful scarves and the 'Beautiful Women in Oncology' initiative takes place, with make-up artists on hand to offer advice to ill women.

Another case from Italy that is particularly symbolic, as well as being structurally more composite than the individual stories of cancer bloggers, is that of Salvatore Iaconesi. Robotic engineer, hacker, TED and Eisenhower Fellow, upon discovering he had a brain tumour, Iaconesi decided to put his own medical records online using Open Source. He created a website (la-cura.it) where he invites people to give their own opinion, or simply react using personal accounts, poetry, works of art, scientific research and so forth. Finally, he recounted this experiment – an Open Source Cure for Cancer – in a book called *La Cura* [*The Cure*], written with his wife Oriana Persico. The online sharing of his cancer diagnosis, by violating 'the most intimate stronghold of privacy, the body, and literally publishing it online, he ripped the cancer from its bureaucracy and isolation, bringing it into society'.[22] A number of words in the text clearly indicate the central role played by digital technologies in the relationship between human beings, illness and end of life:

> It was a call to my peers, to those like me, to join me in my illness. A call to embrace a possibilistic vision of life, the only one to my mind capable of taking illness back into society, saving it from the segregation brought about through medicalization and avoiding it being held in large boxes on the edges of society, ready to be administrated and bureaucratized. A call to take illness back into the thick of life [...] I wanted a *peer-to-peer* cure, one that was ecosystemic, much like life.[23]

In other words, Salvatore chose to use the tools currently offered by the web in order to allow the patient to stay in the 'club of the living', remaining connected to the public space in which he was raised and lives. The integration of his cancer with the flux of life through a peer-to-peer and eco-systemic cure could take place thanks to the messages, almost a million, Salvatore received via email, on his social network profiles, and through the way his initiative had been amplified by national and international newspapers. Fairly sound medical advice, works of art, poetry, simple demonstrations of proximity, detailed scientific research: all this material he received also led to the encounter between Salvatore and the surgeon who cured him.

Beyond a series of technical considerations regarding this experiment, or this 'performance' to use Salvatore's words, the Open Source Cure for Cancer clearly demonstrates the innovative role played by digital technology in terms of our connection with illness. A role that opens up new theoretical and practical frontiers through which we can, firstly, bring our relationship to treatment onto parallel tracks that bring together the complexity of the subjective experience and scientific truth, without falling into a vague relativism of therapeutic methodologies. Secondly, it brings the illness back into the public sphere as an event *integral* to life, implementing the experiment in collective cultural autobiography. By discussing it explicitly in online interactive spaces where each person is a narrative fragment of a global interconnection and can arbitrarily attribute to themselves the image or word they prefer, means diffusing that harmful social attitude that views illness as an 'exception' that is *external* to a life lived as if it were infinite.

Interactive personal diaries, archives for future patients, inter-subjective places in which to express disembodied sentiments without embarrassment: by stitching together the many fragments of words and images, the autobiographical memories of cancer bloggers offer a broader vision when it comes to subjects that are kept outside our daily lives.

However, there is of course no shortage of problems. On the one hand, the absence of a physical presence can lead to superficial and disrespectful behaviour towards the ill person's decision to expose themselves. The case of Italian television presenter Nadia Toffa illustrates this perfectly. In the caption beneath the image of her autobiography shared on Instagram on 22 September 2018, she writes: 'In this book I explain how I managed to turn what everyone considers really bad luck, #cancer, into a gift, an opportunity.' Her followers, in cahoots with the national press, clumsily oversimplify the phrase's content, reducing it to the following misleading message: 'cancer is a gift'. This is followed by an incalculable number of insults and threats which, having been caused by a poor interpretation of the text, accompanied Toffa throughout her illness right up until her death. This case is useful for reminding us that (1) all written text can be superficially misinterpreted, even in cases where its meaning cannot be misconstrued, perhaps due to prejudice towards its author; and (2) that publicly revealing one's own illness touches a raw nerve in those who are used to it being hidden, leading to inevitable repulsion.

On the other hand, those exposing their illness run the real risk of confusing the reality of the illness with its representation if they are not able to attribute the correct significance to the images, words and videos shared, inserted together within a connection that regulates online autobiographical writing. For example, a video by Daniel Edward Thomas could be viewed with the same attitude, and therefore the same detachment, as a series on Netflix.

However, these issues, which can be mitigated through appropriate education on the proper usage of social networks when it comes to social phenomena such as those concerning cancer bloggers, do not diminish the advantages that originate on a subjective level from online autobiographical narratives involving a serious debilitating illness. Confirming this are the increasing number of research studies into Digital Health, which find that healthcare staff are keen to progressively use social networks in order to understand the profiles of the sick, so as to improve communication between doctor and patient.

Facebook: Encyclopedia of the Dead 2.0?

Unfortunately, when cancer bloggers die, as with all of those people who up until that moment have taken part in the grand experiment described by Goldsmith, their accounts seem to be subject to a transformation, going from being interactive autobiographical narratives to encyclopedic texts that remain 'live' and 'active' within the social networks hosting them, as demonstrated by the case of Teresa Calvano. The basis for this metamorphosis can be found in the principle governing *The Encyclopedia of the Dead* imagined in 1983 by author Danilo Kiš: life only becomes whole through death.

When describing *The Encyclopedia of the Dead*, Kiš imagines a fantastical library located in Stockholm. Its rooms, linked by a narrow passageway and each marked with a letter of the alphabet, are all the same. The volumes within them, 'fastened by thick chains to iron rings on the shelves'[24] like in medieval libraries, have a rather peculiar characteristic: they contain extremely detailed information on everything that is excluded from the archives of official culture, considered insignificant and unimportant, and not mentioned in other encyclopedias. Facts that are banal and hold no particular value except for those who made them public, and obviously their relatives, friends and acquaintances. Specifically, this library collects facts regarding the lives of everyday people in order to document their unique and irreplaceable existence and keep it alive in collective memory without making any distinction between a country trader or his wife, a village priest or his bell ringer. As we have said, the only condition for joining the library is that the person must not feature in any other encyclopedia. The birth

and death of each one is preserved here alongside documents
that are relevant to the places they have lived (with detailed
references to the specific climate and geographical conditions
that marked their daily lives), descriptions of the clothes they
wore, every detail of that personal information that enriches
a human life (favourite foods, places visited, books read,
etc.). Finally, there is a detailed summary of the illness that
led to their death and how it developed. Notes are included,
detailing the clothes in which the deceased was buried, the
name of the person who washed the body, even the location
of the tree felled to make the coffin and the name of the
person who chose it. Kiš maintains that the principle guiding
every volume conserved in his imaginary encyclopedia is that
life reaches completion only once it has come to an end.

In this library, any distinction between the significant
and the insignificant, between memory and forgetting is
eliminated. No detail is considered insignificant, nor is
there a hierarchy of events. 'For *The Encyclopedia of the
Dead,* history is the sum of human destinies, the totality of
ephemeral happenings. That is why it records every action,
every thought, every creative breath, every spot height in
the survey, every shovelful of mud, every motion that
cleared a brick from the ruins.'[25] Aleida Assmann says of the
library described by Kiš that it is 'a negative archive of the
"unarchived"'.[26] In fact, he reconstructs a 'counter-memory'
because he attempts to codify a kind of personal memory
that is usually lost once the person who produced it has died.
The task of this library is to offer 'an egalitarian vision of the
world of the dead', therefore 'addressing human injustices'
and affording all humans an equal place in eternity.[27] This
is demonstrated by the young woman who, having travelled
to Stockholm, spends the entire night inside the library to
'put down as much information as possible' on her father's
life. Her aim in those moments of despair is to gather 'some
evidence, for my hours of despair, that my father's life had
not been in vain, that there were still people on earth who
recorded and accorded value to every life, every affliction,
every human existence'.[28] In other words, no life is worthy
of being consigned to oblivion, which, when it prevails
over memory, suggests that those persons who have been

forgotten had lived in vain. The encyclopedia of the dead is the final bulwark against oblivion.

A paradoxical archive of the non-archived. At the end of the 1970s, *The Twenty Days of Turin* by Giorgio De Maria predicted the peculiar characteristics that, thirty years later, would mark the birth and initial development of Facebook as an online location dedicated to the creation of relationships starting from a personal space that is made public (*I will give myself to you, you will give yourself to me*). Danilo Kiš' *The Encyclopedia of the Dead*, in turn, predicted, in the early 1980s, the evolution of Zuckerberg's social network after fifteen years of activity. Facebook seems, in fact, to be the version 2.0 of the encyclopedia of the dead. It currently includes some fifty million profiles belonging to deceased users, each packed with words, images and videos that, when put together, create an equal number of personal biographies. Anyone who accesses one of these profiles is able to create a detailed reconstruction of the dead person's life, and make an inventory of the sentimental relationships, work activities, political beliefs exactly as they developed over time. Indeed, each one holds the necessary details with which to build a substantial picture of the way the deceased developed as a person, their expressive peculiarities, their homes, the places visited on holiday or in their free time, as well as the events of varying importance that marked their existence. Facebook in particular, but also the other social networks that have been used for decades, seem to make possible that egalitarian vision of the world of the dead invoked by Kiš, demonstrating how history truly is a sum of human destinies and a collection of ephemeral events. A website such as MyDeathSpace, for example, which has a collection of pages dedicated to those who have died, each of which contains a hyperlink to the deceased's Facebook profile, confirms (as a middle ground between a virtual cemetery and an encyclopedia of personal stories) the sensation that current digital technologies are radically changing our way of telling stories.[29]

However, the fact that Facebook is also a grand experiment in collective cultural autobiography stops its total identification as an encyclopedia of the dead. Unlike the library described by Kiš, which only contains accounts of the deceased, Facebook currently has a higher number of living users. Predictions by Hachem Saddiki, a researcher in statistics at the University of Massachusetts, indicate 2098 as the year in which the number of profiles of the deceased will overtake those of the living. In a recent study by Oxford University's Oxford Internet Institute, this date is brought forward to 2070, a date reached by using the birthdays of profiles from 2018, which suggest that by 2100 the lives of one and a half billion users will have inevitably come to an end. If Facebook continues to attract users, increasing its number of users at the same rate we have seen up to this point, it could have almost five billion profiles of dead users before the end of the century. It will only truly become an encyclopedia of the dead on the day when Facebook no longer has a single living user, or when the living subscribers are so few that they will benefit from a situation as unprecedented as it is fascinating: they will visit Facebook not to socialize but to visit the digital tombs of the dead, re-reading, re-listening and looking once more at their written and audio-visual memories.

At the same time, Facebook's comparison (albeit partial) to an encyclopedia of the dead diminishes its identification as a grand experiment in collective cultural autobiography. In other words: if in Zuckerberg's social network the living and the dead share the same space, often blending with one another, then it is showing itself to be a hybrid space containing equally hybrid narrative forms. In part it resembles an ongoing autobiographical memory, in part an encyclopedia of the dead 2.0. How do these two narrative modes fit together, modes that characterize (and this must be emphasized) not just Facebook but all social networks?

Autobiographical Memory: Inventing the Past

Whether experiments of collective cultural autobiographies or encyclopedias of the dead: in order to better understand the nature of social networks, we need to take a step back and consider the inescapable condition that (according to Schelling) governs the equivalence between writing the story of one's own life and the brief summary of the history of the universe. Put simply, a clear awareness of the current relationship between the past, the present and the future.

The past is known and the known is only recounted through a process of *reconstruction* that, though aware that temporal duration implies a present that passes and a past that remains, nevertheless rigorously distinguishes between the past and the present, known and exposed, and the future, predicted and prophesized. There is no autobiographical memory that does not entail a backwards movement through time towards what is no longer, starting from a perspective recognized as current, or what is now. The gaze is turned to the past with the single aim of reconstructing it. The present revives the spectres of the past which it preserves in order to turn them towards the future, using them to predict what will be. The content of autobiographical narrative consists, therefore, in a relatively long part of life lived, and therefore irremediably terminated, being considered a totality in which the correlation between single facts and the reconstructed elements takes place according to a particular order or a determined finality. This correlation calls into question subjective memory, the actions of which are summed up by Aleida Assmann in the following way:

> Remembering is basically a reconstructive process, it always starts in the present, and so inevitably at the time when the memory is recalled, there will be shifting, distortion, revaluation, reshaping. In the period between present action and future recall, memory does not wait patiently in its safe house, it has its own energy and is exposed to a process of transformation.[30]

The essentially reconstructive progress of subjective memory depends on its intermittent structure, which never presupposes a permanent presence or, alternatively, a total absence, but the continual alternation between presence and absence. No one remembers what is present, rather they remember that which, temporarily repressed and preserved in a place that cannot be identified with the here and now, sets in motion the processes of dislocation, deformation, alteration, slippage and renewal with which Assmann sums up the characteristics of human memory. Memory can never be compared to a deposit or archive that warehouses and safeguards the details and footprints in an objective way, using an efficient and linear management method. Rather, memory allows for them to be autonomously processed in a way that, regardless of what actually happened, keeps track of the temporary changes and processes of sedimentation to which the events are subjected.

When it comes to autobiographical narrative, we can see this in the dialectic between the narrating I and the narrated I, which, though they partially coincide, also differ from one another. The first not only exists in an earlier time than the second, but also at the end of a cycle or evolution that is the object of its reworking and narrative in memory. The constant flux of life that determines a continuous accumulation of memories and forgotten things, of disappointments and traumas, stops the narrating I and the narrated I from ever fully coinciding. The narrating I already knows what the narrated I does not, and cannot impartially read its life during the reconstruction and representation of its development. A recent psychological study focused on interpreting the answers given by four hundred people over the age of thirty to the question: 'What advice would you give to your younger self?' The overwhelming prevalence of regret ('If I could go back, I wouldn't do X or Y') proves an often radical difference between one's current identity and that of the past, a difference that impedes an impartial judgement of past events.[31]

Furthermore, the continual alternation between presence and absence, and therefore the fundamental mediation of forgetting, block the objective and detailed reconstruction of events that have occurred, causing them to be partially forgotten or repressed. One of the characteristics of subjective memory is precisely the reciprocal implication between remembering and forgetting, by which one makes the other possible. Despite remembering generally having a positive value attached to it, with forgetting deemed negative, the two actions are closely bound and, as Assmann states:

> they organize the changeable rhythms of our conscience. Everything that we remember has had to disappear from the surface of our conscience for some time. *Remembering can be in no way compared to a live recording of knowledge* [...] rather, it is akin to a 're-turn' or a 're-cognition' beyond the

pauses in time. Remembering takes on weight and significance when it overcomes a temporal distance and a phase of
absence of awareness.[32]

Without forgetting, any reconstruction of the past would take
exactly the same time as the event being reconstructed, generating such paralysis as to make both its evaluation and its
retelling prohibitive. A recent study carried out by researchers
at the Universities of Buenos Aires and Cambridge, whose
results were published in *Nature Communications*, proves
the essential importance of forgetting, which is not a passive
activity but an active one: the quantity of stimuli we receive
every moment does not match our brain's capacity to process
it, engaged as it is in the active task of not registering all
information, while at the same time selecting that which has
already registered. In other words, the very act of remembering implies an act of forgetting.[33]

It follows that, in the reconstruction of the past, the
imagination also plays an essential role, its principal function
consisting of offering up the events that have taken place once
more in a new way, arbitrarily adding information, desires
and aspirations that are often anachronistic and plucked
from thin air. As psychologist Frederic Bartlett observes,
remembering is not the reactivation of isolated traces that
are fixed and lifeless, but a fantastical reconstruction conditioned by the interests and objectives the individual develops
within the time and socio-cultural context in which they
currently live.[34] In this sense, we should rethink the words
Samantha offers to Theodore Twombly in the film *Her*: the
past is only a story that we tell ourselves. Paradoxically, what
has happened in the past, when observed from a present
perspective, has never 'actually' happened. It 'only comes
into being insofar as we refer to it [...] Nothing appears more
natural than the formation of the past – it comes into being
through the passing of time. Thus, by tomorrow, today will
be history in the form of yesterday.'[35] This is why Italo Svevo
concludes:

> But the past is always new: as life proceeds it changes, because
> parts of it that may have once seemed to have sunk into
> oblivion rise to the surface and others vanish without a trace

because they have come to have such slight importance. The present conducts the past in the way a conductor conducts an orchestra. It wants these particular sounds – and no others. That explains why the past may at times seem very long and at times very short. It thunders forth and murmurs *pianissimo*. The only part of it that is highlighted is the part that has been summoned up to illumine, and to distract us from, the present.[36]

One of the most famous examples of an autobiography based on the link between memory and imagination is *Poetry and Truth* by Goethe, divided into four parts published respectively in 1811, 1812, 1814 and 1833. Each of these is in turn subdivided into five books, in which only the first 26 years of Goethe's life are narrated, despite the fact that he was 62 when the first part was published. Accused of having recounted his own personal events in an untruthful way (as demonstrated by the concept of 'poetry' being placed before that of 'truth'), Goethe responds that it is not possible to reconstruct the facts of the past objectively by basing them solely on mnemonic ability. Imagination and fantasy are equally fundamental elements, particularly in reference to events whose outcome we discover after the fact. In other words: it is impossible for Goethe to write about himself without adding poetic invention to the 'truth'. In this combination of poetry and truth lies a creative impulse that is used incessantly internally and externally, and which constitutes the lynchpin of existence and the disbanding of its contradictions. According to Goethe, this creative impulse demonstrates how we must never consider any detail without an implicit and symbolic reference to the totality, meaning a totalizing gaze is necessary in order to grasp the truth of autobiographical events.

In agreement with Goethe is Jonathan Gottschall, who briefly describes a series of autobiographies in which an erroneous reconstruction of events is caused either by forgetting (*The Night of the Gun* by David Carr) or the more arbitrary desire to invent (*Surviving with Wolves* by Misha Defonseca). According to Gottschall, autobiographies should be located in the library and bookshop shelves dedicated to narrative fiction. Memorialists do not tell real stories, but credible ones: 'a life story is a carefully shaped narrative that is replete with strategic forgetting and skilfully spun meanings'.[37]

To all this we add a final fundamental characteristic that defines autobiographical narrative: its provisory nature. The narrator is themselves involved in the (ongoing) plot of their life. All content within their autobiographical narrative is, therefore, conditioned by the open horizon of expectations, even when it refers to a particular time frame, as happens with Goethe's work. Far from occupying a fixed position within a world that is merely represented, the narrator (as Jean Baudrillard observes) is constantly 'trapped in a senseless distribution, an endless cycle impelled by death',[38] caught in the folds of an unobjectifiable world that influences and changes him endlessly. Being 'trapped in a senseless distribution' means relating to the world from a place of reciprocal exchange, hybridization, contamination between elements that are never the same, that never correspond entirely. The fact that the 'endless cycle' in which the narrator of the self finds themselves is 'impelled by death' implies both an inextricable interweaving of living and dying, and the constant return of any vital movement to a static equilibrium and an unspecified duration whose end point is the end of their existence. Only the narrator's death guarantees the completion of the autobiography, conferring an ultimate form on the narrated life. But, from the moment of their death, the narrator is clearly no longer able to have the final word, in the first person, in their autobiographical narrative, which, once death has occurred, becomes an encyclopedic text as Danilo Kiš has shown us. We must not forget it: life only becomes whole through death.

Disinterred Bodies: Social Networks and Data Flows as Archives

The descriptions of the mechanisms of autobiographical memory, starting with the suggestion made by Schelling, now allow us to understand why social networks cannot be fully identified with either autobiographical narratives or encyclopedias of the dead, as they are actually an unprecedented hybrid of both.

If we were to limit ourselves to a superficial interpretation of the temporal dynamics that characterize various online locations, we might believe that social networks faithfully reproduce the same temporal dialectic as is found in the offline dimension: the alternation between the present that passes and the past that remains. In fact, Facebook, Twitter, Instagram, et al. all constantly combine the fleetingness of the instant with the static nature of the present.

The fleetingness of the instant. Every social network is governed by the unwritten rule that whatever is a trending topic today will be obsolete by tomorrow. Take the rabid online debate on the differences of social class unleashed the day after publication of Michele Serra's column *Amaca* in Italian newspaper *La Repubblica*, on 20 April 2018. Serra attributed a series of instances in Italy of high-school students intimidating their teachers to the social and cultural backgrounds of those involved, thus establishing a questionable relationship of cause and effect. Facebook, Twitter and Instagram were literally flooded by an incalculable number of comments in favour of and against Serra's interpretation. Rivers of words, often bubbling over into general hysteria and gratuitous insult, that nevertheless dried up over the course of a few hours. The continual production of data makes online events occur at lightning speed and the swapping of information and images frenzied. The facts that overlap in a diverse and badly organized way are ephemeral and unstable. One day everyone is talking about Elisa being murdered by Massimo, filling social network profiles with references to the victim using specific hashtags, the next, the public's attention switches to the controversy over the filling for Bolognese tortellini and the absence of Ilary Blasi in the commemorative episode of the TV programme *Le Iene* dedicated to Nadia Toffa. It is no coincidence that the structure of these 'stories' is based on live streaming and visibility for no longer than 24 hours. Comparing the tweets that run down the computer screen to the stock quotes shown continuously on the Times Square news zipper, Goldsmith notes how posts on social networks acquire value in rapid succession: 'the more blasts you broadcast with greater frequency, the more effective they are until, like so many little shards, they accumulate into a grand narrative of life. Yet, as soon as they appear, they're pushed off the screen and evaporate.'[39]

The *staticity of the present*. Beneath the surface of a sudden present hides a mysteriously static and stagnant past ready to resurface at any moment in order to stop itself being archived definitively. Michele Serra, Elisa, the filling of Bolognese tortellini, Ilary Blasi: once they've left our screens they do not evaporate but remain squarely in place. The obsolete character they assume is, in fact, only an appearance. They continue to wander alongside whatever has replaced them, ready to return, relevant, at any moment. The mechanisms used by the aforementioned Facebook sections of On This Day and Memories prove this. The title 'On This Day' is, in particular, a perfect example of this staticity if we focus our attention on 'today'. Just think of the repeated example of my sharing the ticket from the Nirvana concert: though this becomes obsolete from the moment in which it is substituted by other publications, it becomes current once more each time I decide to repost it, setting in motion a mechanism that will make it always new thanks to the interactions it produces, which change the narrative each time.

Fleetingness of the instant and staticity of the present, a present that passes and a past that remains. There is, however, a fundamental element that clearly distinguishes between the temporal dialectic of social networks and that of the offline reality: the first is physically recorded, and as such is fixed and objectified. Through this recording, every action, every word, every dialogical exchange becomes an object, a document, a fixed fact. Unlike the flux that defines our time offline, this recording brings an inevitable contemporaneity to the continuous production of new data and the constant permanence of those who, their moment having passed, should, in theory, be eliminated or obsolete at least.[40]

In his book *Present Shock*, Douglas Rushkoff maintains that digital technologies have fused together two different forms

of temporality: stored time and flowing time. The first needs
to be decompressed and its connection created from information and symbols. The second happens in the instant and
always requires our presence. Rushkoff compares stored time
to a pond, which, because it is made up of water that does not
flow and cannot be consumed, remains stagnant. Its staticity
ensures, however, that a living ecosystem is born within it.
Conversely, he compares flowing time to a stream, which,
unlike the pond, is defined by its continuous, unbroken
movement. As it flows it can, over time, carve out a path
in the rock, but this stops the birth of any new ecosystems
or cultures within it. 'The pond creates change within itself
by staying still. The stream creates change beyond itself by
remaining in motion.'[41]

If we compare the characteristics of the pond and the
stream to the social networks we use every day, we reach the
following conclusion: 'the pond contains its content, while the
stream uses the earth around itself as its content. Likewise,
our informational content comes to us both as ponds and
streams – stored data and flows of data.'[42] For example, with
its staticity the encyclopedia suggests stored time. Its intrinsic
value therefore depends on the durability of its contents. 24/7
informational programming instead reminds us of time that
flows, and the autobiographical activity developed within
social networks. Its value depends on the constancy with
which information is updated. The problem arises when
recording leads us to identify and confuse data flows with
archives, treating the former as if they were the latter.

With regard to this, Rushkoff maintains that we are
living in the age of *present shock*, which has generated a
'culture [that becomes] an entropic, static hum of everybody
trying to capture the slipping moment. Narrativity and
goals are surrendered to a skewed notion of the real and the
immediate; the Tweet; the status update.'[43] Consequently, he
insists that this confusion between data flows and archives
not only lays the foundations for a life lived in the present
continuous, but also forces us to dedicate the same time
and attention to archived information (i.e. a book) and that
which is fluid (all news informational programming), with
no attempt to keep them separate. This kind of superficial
behaviour is magnified when certain kinds of information

display characteristics of both the archive and the flow. One example of this is electronic mail, as arriving emails can (depending on the circumstances) be interpreted as both a data flow and a collection of archived information.

The confusion between data flows and archives, beyond any reference to the multiple kinds of information, leads to the paradoxical staticity of every shared piece of data. This translates into the exact opposite of what Aleida Assmann asserts: that memory is comparable to a live recording of knowledge. It follows, then, that in the absence of a clear distinction between that which is and that which has been, the past, the story we tell our followers by recording it online is submitted to a continual process of *exhumation* that is not metaphorical but literal. This is not simply reposting an event for present memory that, having taken place in the past and uploaded in real time on Facebook (for example), is recognized as having come to a definite end within its temporal compartment. Rather, what happens is a genuine digital disinterment of the body. What appeared buried in memory is returned to the present intact. The material container, permanent and indestructible, within which every lived experience is registered and preserved ensures that these experiences never degrade or decompose. This digital disinterment of the body is then facilitated by the fact that every social profile coincides with:

- *One* of the innumerable digital identities in which we have multiplied our unique psycho-physical presence. Its body, as we know, is made up of the message (words, images, videos) that the body transmits with and to others.
- The *collection* of traces, information and data that constitutes a digital archive of our memories.

In other words, the collection of digital footprints, information and data contained in one social media account, while it inevitably creates a deposit for our memories, also represents the actual 'physical presence' of the account owner. We have seen this in our examination of cancer bloggers. The account owner's biological death does not imply the digital death of their identity, which lives on inside these accounts. Once the deceased has been cremated, there is not then an automatic digital cremation of those identities they have scattered throughout the online dimension. These continue to 'live' autonomously and be 'active', even in the absence of the person who produced, controlled and updated them from behind the computer screen. The interaction between data and digital identities is therefore also posthumous.

In the specific case of cancer bloggers who have died, this means the positive transformation of an autobiographical memory into an encyclopedia 2.0 where both a collection of precious memories and a lesson of sizeable pedagogical value can be found. However, in general, the excessive quantity of the present that we entrust to the past, from the moment in which it becomes a story we tell our followers, generates the conditions that allow the past to emancipate itself and become an autonomous, independent reality. This situation, as we will see in the following chapter, is both a technological opportunity for reaching goals that, until now, have belonged to the realms of science-fiction (total recall and digital immortality), and an issue for everyone who, unable to escape their past, views the internet as a melancholy container of regret, leaving them imprisoned by nostalgia for an ostensibly golden time that entirely consumes the future.

3
Total Recall, Digital Immortality, Retromania

Becoming the Database of Ourselves: Lifelogging and Video-Camera Memory

The confusion between data flows and digital archives, between moments that follow one another in frenzied succession and those that never pass, triggers in the minds of certain scientists the categorical imperative to fill all the space! On the one hand, we accumulate an historically unprecedented number of personal memories on a daily basis, narrating every single autobiographical experience in minute detail. On the other, we place these memories within a digital space where the constant disinterment of the body produces a total co-existence between the past and the present, rendering the past independent, a world in its own right. Why, then, not make the most of these peculiarities and create a permanent and omni-pervasive presence that eliminates any absence or interval of latency? In other words, why not attempt to create *total recall*? Much like an objective archive, this would halt both the irreversible deletion of all traces and their momentary concealment, ensuring we would never again forget a thing.

Gordon Bell and Jim Gemmell attempted to provide a clear response to these two questions back in 1998, at a time in which the real and the virtual were still clearly viewed as two reciprocally separate entities. The detailed account of their experience can be found in their book *Total Recall*, published in 2009 and whose preface was written by a certain Bill Gates. In the final years of the twentieth century, these two Microsoft researchers were laying the foundations for an ambitious project called MyLifeBits. Initially aimed at digitalizing books written by Bell, MyLifeBits quickly set its sights on a much more ambitious objective: lifelogging, the minute-by-minute recording of one's daily life. Bell and Gemmell want to record everything they see, feel, and learn and then archive it in digital format.

Their reference model for the project was Memex, whose characteristics are described by Vannevar Bush, director of the Federal Office of Scientific Research and Development, in the essay, *We May Think*, published in the *Atlantic Monthly* in 1945, 'when electronic computers were actually multistory buildings'.[1] Memex, a contraction of the term *memory expansion*, is a device aimed at storing the books, records and communications in one's possession. Considered a precursor to the personal computer, it was a kind of desk with tilted, back-lit screens placed on top, onto which it was possible to project one's personal material for ease of reading. The desk also had a keyboard and a set of buttons and levers. All of its content was acquired through inserted microfilms . Also included was a transparent slab on which handwritten documents, photographs, memorandums, etc. were placed. Once an object had been placed on the slab, it could be photographed simply by moving a lever. Another way of inserting material into the Memex was to wear a photo camera that would automatically capture images of the objects.

Bell and Gemmell believe that we are now ready for a tool capable of expanding human memory, one that bridges the disproportionate gap between biological and digital memories. The fragility of our biological memory, whose degeneration due to Alzheimer's disease in old age is increasingly common, proves to be a lucrative business for the industry dedicated to producing medicinal herbs and food supplements that claim to strengthen it. According to the two scholars, in 2007, the US sector of brain-fitness apps and neurosoftware registered a turnover of $225 million. So, it is worth devising alternative solutions for people's mnemonic requirements. Putting to one side *procedural* memory, which deals with *how* to do things such as ride a bicycle or tie one's shoelaces, MyLifeBits focuses on *semantic* memory, the part that codifies meaning, definitions and concepts, and on the *episodic* or *autobiographical* memory that, as we have already seen, deals with facts and events in our lives. The latter is defined by Bell and Gemmell as 'subjective, patchy, emotion-tinged, ego-filtered, impressionistic, and mutable'.[2] It reduces every attempt at an objective reconstruction of the past to a tale of mere fantasy due to the primary role played by forgetting. It deforms, constricts and modifies past time and experiences in various different ways, due to the emotions and imagination through which they are constantly filtered. When, for example, we repeat the story of a lived experience more than once, we tend to overlap our initial memory with that of the times in which we retold the story. In doing so we contaminate the initial memory (itself already tenuous) with the memory of its repetition, including the specific words used to recount the experience and interactions by those who, upon hearing the story, intervened, offering pause for thought and new interpretations.

Unlike those who believe forgetting to be a fundamental biological activity, and therefore define remembering and forgetting as two equally necessary processes, the two Microsoft researchers reason in the opposite way: they view forgetting in pathological terms, seeing it as a negation of memory, an illness that requires a technological invention to cure us.

The suppression of gaps in episodic or autobiographical memory implies, therefore, the strengthening of digital memory, which is always 'objective, dispassionate, prosaic, and unforgivingly accurate'.[3] Its task is to ensure that autobiographical memory is no longer an unstable reconstruction of varyingly plausible fragments belonging to a finished era, but the objective and exhaustive representation of everything that has been experienced. Lifelogging essentially has the task of making digital memory akin to the 'playing back a mental videotape in your mind's home theatre system'. Like the lens of a video camera, that belonging to digital memory is not plagued by jolts or the batting of eyelids, 'never drifts into daydream or does a double take. A camera will record an hour of pedestrian cross-walk traffic with the same fidelity as it will witness an hour of bloody genocide.'[4] These traits allow us to hypothesize the attribution of an objective content to all lived experiences, so as to have at our future disposal digital memories that always remain the same, that are capable of halting the disappearance of our organic ones.

The authors lay out three phases of work for the creation of a memory that has the same traits as a video camera. The first consists of making a digital copy of everything that, having belonged to past eras and as such not recorded on video, is nevertheless conserved within material objects and in analogue formats. The second involves the active creation of a software to actually carry out the *lifelogging*, starting to record on camera everything that is seen, felt and done on a daily basis, acquiring every detail without discarding a single thing. Bell writes, 'We started tracking all kinds of things: the number of mouse and keyboard clicks, every time a document opened, every window shown on my PC screen, and the history of my music playback.'[5] The level of detail required by the recording pushes the two researchers to wear, at all times, tiny microphones, video cameras, location monitors and any other tool necessary for ensuring that everything that is seen and experienced is automatically recorded, photographed and transformed into objective fact, much like the content of a film. The third and final phase involves the choice of exactly how to build an archive of memories that can be easily consulted and that is able to provide the necessary tools with which to create a personal library of the words, images and videos as they are accumulated. This is thought to be the most complicated phase, as we are yet to find the perfect way to carefully manage the vast amount of material, data and information conserved over the years. Goldsmith suggests that 'Like quilting, archiving employs the obsessive stitching together of many small pieces into a larger vision, a personal attempt at ordering a chaotic world.'[6]

Once these three phases of work have been carried out, each person will have a total memory, making them 'the librarian, archivist, cartographer, and curator of [their] life'.[7]

Bell and Gemmell maintain that if this kind of *e-memory* can be preserved in the cloud, placing it at our disposal 24/7, every human being will become a walking, talking version of Wikipedia or Google, or a database of their own personal experiences, which can be projected onto the walls of the office or the kitchen table, making our memories and lived experiences forever present. Never again will anyone forget the name of someone they've just met, or leave home without their car keys. Our way of learning and studying school subjects will be completely revolutionized, the nature of psychotherapy sessions will change along with bets between friends and testifying in court. Arguments between married couples will employ objective data that will make a subjective interpretation of events unfeasible. It will become simpler for doctors and patients to communicate with fewer misunderstandings in the case of illness. Each person will acquire the capacity to structure and organize their own information in advance, with a view to archiving in a way that allows its constant reuse. And, finally, a new way of remembering past events in our lives will be produced: 'Think of how nice it would be to have recordings of childhood conversations with your best friend, or a complete audio library of the millions of priceless things your kids said when they were toddlers.'[8]

The lifelogging imagined by Bell and Gemmell is, essentially, the real-life version of the SQUID (Superconductive Quantum Interference Device) unit imagined in Kathryn Bigelow's film, *Strange Days* (1995) and that allows Lenny Nero (Ralph Fiennes) to relive the passionate nights spent with his ex-girlfriend Faith (Juliette Lewis) as many times over as he wants. Encounters that were recorded live and conserved in numerous clips. It is also the perfect tool with which to create Rememory, the video-memory that is used to create a montage of the deceased's life and is projected at their funeral in the fantasy brought to the screen by Omar Naim in *The Final Cut* (2004). Parents have a kind of 'black box' or mnemonic chip called Zoe implanted into the brains of their newborn children, through which everything they see and hear over the course of their lives is recorded. Alan W. Hakman (Robin Williams) has the job of selecting the content found in Zoe when someone dies to ensure the video-memory does not contain any skeletons in the cupboard, respecting the requests of the family members who commissioned the work. MyLifeBits seems, as such, destined to create new kinds of (solipsistic) enjoyment and work. For Bell and Gemmell, remembering is objectively equivalent to a live recording of knowledge.

The Memobile: *From Total Recall to Digital Immortality*

Beyond their specific project, Bell and Gemmell are convinced that in just ten years' time (so by 2019 to be exact) lifelogging will have become a common practice, given further developments in digital technology. They imagine the imminent possibility of having multiple mobile devices connected to one another to create a valid system for the collection and management of digital memories, within a container that automatically records, memorizes, indexes and archives every lived experience.

Though their prediction didn't quite hit the mark, the two American scholars did come very close. The current equivalent of MyLifeBits is, in fact, that which Anna Reading defines (not without irony) as a *memobile*, a neologism bringing together the words *me*, *mobile* and *meme* ('a unit of cultural information that is repeatedly transmitted and can self-propagate rather like a virus').[9] The *memobile* is none other than the smartphone used by each of us on a daily basis, embracing it enthusiastically from its initial development as Simon, designed by IBM in 1992 and available on the market in 1993. The smartphone, if we consider its current traits, allows us to access that collection of personal and collective memories we listed in Chapter 1, no matter where we are or what time it is. It also gathers together a significant amount of data and information produced automatically, with which it is fairly easy to work out how its owner spends their days: the number of steps taken during their walks, the cities, restaurants and anywhere else they may have visited thanks to geo-location, the songs they listen to, the websites they visit, and everything that is automatically produced with the use of any single application. A collection of data that, as we have seen, helps Moritz to second-guess the moves of his love rival in the television series, *How to Sell Drugs Online (Fast)*, and allows any parent, once that collection is integrated by images and videos held on smartphones and social networks, to create a Rememory of their children, even after their death. Every parent today has the tools with which to create an amateur film on their children's lives, from the moment they are born onwards. Dataism, or the religion of data discussed by Harari, involves precisely this awareness that the registration of all this daily material is leading to the human being's gradual substitution with computerized algorithms capable of autonomously redefining their very life experience.

What we are still lacking in this quest to create a perfect link between MyLifeBits and our daily *memobile* is a rational system for organizing documents shared and footprints left online, one that allows the smartphone to autonomously rationalize and coordinate the associative links bound to our lives, to reconstruct the accumulated knowledge and prudently manage the only acceptable form of forgetting: namely, the momentary exclusion of data that is not required in a particular situation. Facebook, for example, is trying to transform its users into a living database of their existence through the invention of the sections On This Day and Memories, and its future plans for a universal inventory of all the data users have shared from the moment it was invented by Zuckerberg. For now, we still have the objective difficulty of bridging the gap between digital archives and physical ones whose content is selected through careful evaluation.

With regard to the plausible realization of Bell and Gemmell's project, Kevin Kelly is certain that the next developments in social networks and the internet more generally will include a mechanism that will allow immersive environments and virtual realities to browse freely through previous states: 'anything digital will have undo and rewindability as well as remixing'.[10] So we will become accustomed to our lives undergoing the same change brought to the television screen by the video recorder: with the recording and storage of every single experience, we can use the rewind button on our own *memobiles*. We will be able to relive our first kiss or PhD vivas infinite times over, in the same way that, today can we listen over and over to the guitar solo in the middle of a rock song. Like the two Microsoft researchers, Kelly is also convinced that the availability of an objective digital memory will radically transform our lives: 'The social etiquette around recall will be in flux; private conversations are likely to be off-limits [...] more and more of what happens in public will be recorded – and re-viewable – via phone cams, dashboard-mounted webcams on every car, and streetlight-mounted surveillance cams.'[11]

There are people who are even trying to include our dreams in our total future memory. The scholar Daniel Oldis, author of the book *The Lucid Dream Manifesto*, together with a team of researchers from different US universities, wants to find out whether it is possible to record our dreams, so as to be able to reproduce them as if they were films. In order to include dreams in the lifelogging project, they are coming up with tools that register both the motor behaviour of the dreamer and the words they say as they sleep, thus creating a detailed inventory of our dream activity. This is joined by experiments involving the recording of images produced in our brains as we sleep. For example, Yukiyasu Kamitani, university professor in Kyoto (Japan), is conducting research that focuses on the reconstruction of the images we see as we dream, using magnetic resonance imaging and a *deep learning* algorithm.[12]

The future possibility of a digital memory that, much like a videocamera, fills in the gaps and blanks created by forgetting and dream, and that equates memory with a live recording of knowledge, leads us to another idea expressed by Gemmell and Bell: the step from lifelogging to digital immortality. According to the two scholars, the path towards the eternalization of data must follow these four steps:

1. An initial digitalization of media content with regard to the inheritance of the deceased;
2. The use of new digital technology to integrate and amplify the material accumulated by the deceased;
3. The creation of an avatar of the deceased with which to make the recorded material active and dynamic, ensuring that this definitively takes the place of the person who is no longer with us biologically;

4. Ensuring the avatar's total autonomy, meaning that it will be able to learn and update. In this way, the avatar will be able to distance itself gradually from the person who initially created it as their digital ghost. An individual's collection of memories will therefore become an *other*, entirely autonomous person.[13]

The ultimate outcome of a total digital memory that also includes our night-time dreams can only be the definitive emancipation of memory from the person who produced them in the first place and the consequent independence of our *memobiles* from us, their owners. The *memobiles* will be capable of representing us eternally as they are equipped with all the data and information needed to reconstruct and substitute us post-mortem. In other words, if the autonomy of the past as a material reality that co-exists with the present unites with the multiplication of biological identities in our multiple digital Is, we inevitably arrive at a radical transformation of both our way of remembering and the relationship each individual has with the life and death.

The Memory Remains: *The Life of Memories Post-Mortem*

The logical endpoint of total recall's struggle against forgetting, aimed at filling all the available space and providing us with an *e-memory* free from any biological fragility, is the project of digital immortality. Since the beginning of time, every invention aimed at preserving and prolonging life by somehow recording that which is dying or has already gone, has also been a more or less symbolic attempt to oppose both that thing's absence and the acceptance of their passing. Forgetting and death share the same unhappy task: the uninterrupted production of absences and empty spaces.

This relationship between forgetting and death is clearly pointed out by Irvin D. Yalom who, while establishing a clinical link between various cases of depression and the terror felt when faced with death, notes how this terror also includes an awareness of forgetting. Quoting Milan

Kundera, he insists that what terrifies us about death is not the loss of the future but the loss of the past. Forgetting is, in fact, an early form of death as it symbolically forewarns us several times a day about the event that will take place when this life has reached its definitive end.[14] This concept is reiterated in an equally clear way by Jan Assmann, when he describes death as both 'the rupture between yesterday and today' and the moment in which 'the choice to obliterate or preserve must be considered'.[15] Only once it has come to an irreversible end can life assume the form of the past on which the culture of memory is built. This is also demonstrated by Danilo Kiš' *The Encyclopedia of the Dead* and, in particular, the young woman who, having entered the fantastical library in Stockholm, spends the night copying the book dedicated to her father so as not to lose him to eternal oblivion.

In one of the notes written in preparation for the (unfinished) book that should have created the weapon with which to vanquish death (!), Elias Canetti notes what he believes to be a 'notable phrase of Schelling's', written in a letter sent by the German philosopher to his friend Georgii at Easter in 1811: 'we must not settle for the generic persistence of our dead, we would rather preserve their personalities in their entirety'.[16] This notable phrase of Schelling's unwittingly captures the fundamental objective of any modern technological invention aimed at obviating the voids generated by both forgetting and death. The deceased has always immediately embodied, the minute death occurs, the presence of an absence. While death imposes absence on presence, human beings try incessantly to fill that absence with the thought of a presence, making the memory of the dead a way of spiritually bringing them back to life, in the absence of more effective solutions. They attempt, therefore, to provide the absence and its posthumous thought with a material content, filling the empty space with the objects of memory. As we know, Walter Benjamin used the expression 'the relic secularized' to describe the completion of the 'experience'. Indeed, it aims to make tangibly present that which cannot be present in any other way. And from this comes 'the increasing self-alienation of the person who inventories his past as a dead possession'.[17] Every object-memory is forced to reckon with an irrepressible ambiguity that is in its very nature: the moment it is placed alongside what it represents in order to make it present once more, it becomes both incapable of identifying with it and, at the same time, unable to distinguish itself from it entirely.

Now, as technology evolves, a lack of satisfaction with a generic persistence of the dead in thoughts or the object-memory mutates into an ambitious attempt actually to preserve their personality in its entirety. We begin by using photography to ensure their image defies the laws of completion, as Roland Barthes and Susan Sontag have taught us. This is then followed shortly after by the preservation of their voices with the invention of the phonograph. The latter's inventor, Thomas Edison, is explicit in his desire to combine the creation of artificial life and a summoning of the dead. In an anonymous article from 1896, entitled *Voices of the Dead*, the invention of the phonograph is hailed as a victory over death. Indeed, the Grim Reaper appears to lose some of his sting the moment human beings (thanks to technology) were able to record, and therefore keep with them forever, the voices of those who had died and who continue to talk despite lacking a physical manifestation. A few years later, in his novel *Ulysses*, James Joyce has Leopold Bloom commenting to himself that a gramophone should be placed in every grave, or at least in every house. That way, after Sunday lunch, it could be turned on so everyone could hear their great-grandfather's voice. 'Remind you of the voice like the photograph reminds you of the face. Otherwise you couldn't remember the face after fifteen years, say.'[18] Preserving voices and images does not, however, provide enough relief. Guy Debord maintains, with regard to the gradual widespread use of television, that by changing the real world into moving images we are ensuring that those images inevitably become real beings that acquire their own unique autonomy from whatever they represent. Television and radio, by seducing our eyes and ears, shape a reality in which various technological mediums trade face-to-face dialogue for representation from a safe distance, physically distinguishing that second world from the one we live in.[19]

It must be said, however, that the doubling produced by instruments such as the phonograph, television and radio allows us only partially to preserve the personalities of those who have died. It makes a dialogue with the dead possible but the living are tasked with managing both sides of the conversation. This suggests that Socrates' well-known objection to the use of writing, whose only function (shared with painting) consists in refreshing the memory of someone who is already familiar with the content, still stands. The impression of having with us someone who has gone, as if able to live and speak, is diminished by the certainty that the recorded words are unable to respond to the questions being asked. At most they 'always say only one and the same thing', maintaining a 'solemn silence'.[20] The importance of this attempt at dialogue, however, no matter how solipsistic it may appear, is well proven by John Durham Peters:

> The call must contain or anticipate the response. Our communication with the dead may never reach them, but such elliptical sending is as important as circular reciprocity. [...] Perhaps all dialogue involves each partner's enacting the response of the other. [...] That I cannot engage in dialogue with Plato or the Beatles does not demean the contact I have with them. Such contact may be hermeneutic and aesthetic rather than personal or mutual. I may have to supply all the replies they might make to my queries – rather like the contact I have with the universe. Or with myself.[21]

The fact I cannot partake in a dialogue with Plato or the Beatles does not demean the contact I have with them. Take, as an example of Peters' pertinent observation, Itaru Sasaki, the 74-year old Japanese gardener who installed a phone booth in his garden in Otsuchi in Iwata prefecture, on a hill overlooking the Pacific Ocean. The phone booth contains a disconnected rotary telephone that allows the relatives of victims of the tsunami that struck Otsuchi on 11 March 2011 to call the dead. Sasaki came up with the idea in order to 'talk' to his cousin who had died a few years earlier, entrusting his thoughts to the symbolic telephone, which are carried to the other side by the wind.

Today's digital technology, inserting itself in the space between the imaginary dialogue with Plato and the Beatles, and the recognized value of this contact, aims to make possible what had up until now been impossible: giving a voice and a body to the dead, emancipating their digital memories. It is this that allows Sasaki's cousin to answer his relative's phone call. If it seems plausible today to defeat forgetting by substituting a faltering autobiographical memory with an objective archive, and therefore with total recall, it is equally plausible to avoid death by making personal memories independent from their owner. The present day works in favour of this possibility, as never before have the human sciences been so quiet with regard to death, giving the impression that it is possible to live *ad libitum*, keeping any notion of the end at bay. The 'strange yet significant' nature of our time, which establishes a displacement between 'the discussion of death in books, which is still prolific, and actual death, which is shameful and not to be talked about',[22] is also reflected in the widespread refusal to mourn, which, unlike in the past, sees the living held to strict rules, keeping their sadness and tears for those who have died private. As Philippe Ariès writes: 'During the course of one generation the situation has been reversed: what had always been required by individual conscience or social obligations is now forbidden; what had always been forbidden is now required. It is no longer correct to display one's grief, nor even to appear to feel any.'[23]

Given that we pretend to live as if we will never die, why then not aim for genuine digital immortality? A positive answer to this query brings together the project of total recall and the goals of transhumanism. 'Man remaining man, but transcending himself, by realizing new possibilities of and for his human nature',[24] writes Julian Huxley, brother of the famous author Aldous, in his book *New Bottles for New Wine* (1957), in which he uses the term 'transhumanism' for the first time. He wants to show 'a new kind of existence' on which the human capacity for *self-transcendence* must converge once we are aware of our own fundamental limits. Huxley's hopes for humanity are borne of his fear (evidenced at the same time by another biologist, Jean Rostand) that we will not be able to evolve if we simply make do with our nature and the limits this imposes. We must, therefore, bring about a new organic change, autonomously and independently of the natural context in which we live. A change that will demonstrate our difference from all other living beings, taking our ability to exercise free will to its fullest extent. According to transhumanists, modern innovations in technology, science, medicine and engineering mean that we can and must rebuild ourselves artificially without having to respect any biological rule or law, and overcome any resistance to powerful technology becoming widespread. Exactly as desired by the advocates of total recall.

Mind-Uploading *as a Declaration of Independence by Memory*

We can clearly see several similarities between the ambitions of the transhumanists, who want a human being like them who is also capable of transcending themselves, and the automatization of digital memories.

From a metaphorical perspective. Of the many images used in literature and philosophy to describe the mechanisms of human memory, and in particular the phenomenon of motivated forgetting, a recurrent one is that of the actions of freezing and defrosting. Motivated forgetting usually refers to a form of forgetting that affects those memories not removed from memory but momentarily repressed, thus allowing them to be newly available in any given future moment. In her autobiographical novel, *Still Alive*, Ruth Klüger recounts a situation in which she struggles to remember a name dating back to the Nazi era. As the memory becomes increasingly vivid, Klüger describes how, at the beginning, 'It's like a dish that one takes out of the freezing compartment, with no smell and no taste. As it thaws, it gives off a gentle aroma. From quite a distance away, I try it – just a taster. Because it was frozen and has now thawed, it has retained the scent of the February wind in 1945, when everything went well for us.'[25]

The mechanism of freezing and defrosting, metaphorically applied here to the phenomenon of motivated forgetting, also regulates the various immortalizing activities promised by cryonic organizations such as Alcor Life Extension and the Cryonics Institute, referenced in Don DeLillo's novel, *Zero K*. Such organizations begin cryonic suspension, the freezing and conservation in liquid nitrogen (around -200°C) of a clinically dead body, in the hope of defrosting it and bringing it back to life in a future where science and technology offer the necessary tools with which to do so. The father of the cryonic movement is Robert Ettinger, author of the 1962 manifesto, *The Prospect of Immortality*, and the first person to experiment with preservation at very low temperatures using the bodies of the recently deceased. The freezing process consists of filling the body with anti-coagulants and anti-freeze agents the moment the doctor declares the patient legally dead, so that the blood can be removed and to avoid the formation of ice crystals that would cause the cells to explode. In this initial phase, the body of the deceased is carefully worked on using techniques reminiscent of those used in embalming. In the second phase, the body that has been prepared and stored at temperatures below -70 degrees centigrade is immersed in a container filled with liquid nitrogen, which should hold it in standby for an indeterminate amount of time.[26] The final objective is exactly that described by Ruth Klüger in relation to motivated forgetting: you pull the odourless body from the freezer and wait for it to defrost, becoming active and fully functioning just as it was before death.

From a realistic perspective. The creators of total recall and the transhumanists converge in their belief that the anthropological mutation currently ongoing due to technological progress consists of the multiplication of a single psychophysical presence into multiple digital I's. At the basis of this convergence is the (more or less deliberate) return to the fundamental principle of traditional Western dualism, understood in its most simple guise: the distinction between the body that dies because it is organic and biodegradable, and the soul (or mind) that lives forever precisely because it is intangible. Such a relationship makes it easier to establish a boundary between an *us* (the souls or minds) and a *them* (the bodies), making it possible to entirely rethink our physical structure as a morphological projection of our existence.[27]

It is no coincidence that the current interpreters of digital technologies and champions of transhumanism are both convinced that the subjective identity can no longer be thought of as unique and homogenous. James Hughes, for example, traces the overcoming of the unique nature of subjective identity to a complete nano-replication of mental processes through which to obtain 'the possibility of identity cloning, distributing one's identity over multiple platforms, sharing of mental components with others, and the merging of several individuals into one identity'.[28] *The Prospect of Immortality*, the aforementioned manifesto of the cryonic movement is even more explicit: 'Let us then cut the Gordian knot by recognizing that identity, like morality, is man-made and relative, rather than natural and absolute.'[29] In other words, if our existence in the world can be reduced down to a problem of identity and containers, it is enough to trade biological identity for multiple digital presences, a 'sum of encounters, relationships, rapport, capable of constantly redrawing the boundaries of a mutant and transitional identitary dimension'.[30] Consequently, it is no longer necessary to think of having a single physical container with which we identify. Biological death can be avoided simply by using the information created from online data: written texts, photographs, videos, work emails, online bank transactions, GPS, music libraries on iTunes and Spotify, and so on. This is the reason Bell and Gemmell hold digital immortality to be the next step after total recall. In fact, they interpret the process of *mind-uploading*, the downloading of our minds into a computer once our organic body has deteriorated, as a declaration of independence by objectively recorded memories. Lived experiences are nothing more than our eternal mind.

The practical terms for reaching digital immortality (which I discuss at length in my book *Online Afterlives*)[31] affect both those who have suffered the loss of someone close to them and those who want never to die. It utilizes a specific posthumous interaction between digital data that remains live and active independently of whoever produced it, and makes possible the autonomy of the past and the independence of memories through the creation of digital spectres known as '*griefbots*'. These come to life using automatic programmes (bot) able to access the web through the same kind of channels used by real humans. They therefore substitute the deceased person of which they are a copy, using repetitive automatisms capable of continuing the life interrupted by death and of bringing comfort to those mourning a loss (grief). The applications for mobile devices such as Eugenia Kuyda's Luka or James Vlahos' *dad-bot*, which offer the living the possibility of chatting actively with a dead friend or relative, are just two of numerous attempts to provide an independent life to digital footprints in order to bring comfort to those who are grieving. The (supposedly exhaustive) entirety of our persona and our behaviour is emancipated, taking our place and keeping our prerogatives eternal. Social networks such as Eter9 and Eterni.me aim instead to create a virtual counterpart of the physical person who, by leaving their own digital footprints within these social networks, gather the memories that will activate and take their place when they die in advance. Both griefbots and their virtual counterparts are, in fact, the post-mortem future of digital memories. They are the collection of our own past memories that, while co-existing with the present time, takes on a life of its own without the burden of the human being who has generated it.

Lurking in the background here are the words spoken by Martha to the digital spectre of Ash, her dead boyfriend, in a famous episode of *Black Mirror*. *Be Right Back* is an episode that had already imagined back in 2013 the kind of digital immortality we have just described: 'You're just a few ripples of you. There's no history to you. You're just a performance of stuff that he performed without thinking and it's not enough.' This brings us back to our discussion of the relationship between the *mukbang* phenomenon and the risk of loneliness. Neither the idea of transforming our memory into an objective video-recording of all lived experiences, nor the desire to gain immortality through the autonomy of recorded memories take into account the fact that those multiple digital identities are nothing more than the technological extension of a unique and unrepeatable psycho-physical identity. Digital reproduction will, as such, always be lacking if it is seen as an alternative to physical existence. 'You're just a few ripples of you' and 'there's no history to you'. In other words, if we do not want to accept the absence generated by forgetting or death, we can console ourselves with a story or a copy, 'but [we must be] careful not to misunderstand the schema', Aleida Assmann concludes, because we must remember that '"most of it is lost" (and it is right that this is the case)'.[32]

In the following passages we will shed some light on what is lost in the case of total recall and a life without death, starting with the famous literary example of Ireneo Funes.

Insomnia Inside a Garbage Heap: Funes, or of a Life that Never Forgets

The most famous literary description of a memory devoid of forgetting is that found in the short story, *Funes The Memorious*, in which Jorge Luis Borges tells the tale of Ireneo Funes. One day, Funes, a peasant from Fray Bentos, is knocked over by a horse. The bang to the head gives him the ability never again to forget a single detail of his lived experience. Up until that moment, he had existed as if in a dream; 'he looked without seeing, listened without hearing, forgetting everything, almost everything'.[33] Following the incident, however, his life changes radically. While others would, at a glance, see three glasses on a table, Funes sees 'all the leaves and tendrils and fruit that make up a grape vine. He knew by heart the forms of southern clouds at dawn on 30 April 1882, and could compare them in his memory with the mottled streaks on a book in Spanish binding he had only seen once.'[34] He not only remembers every leaf of every tree of every mountain, but also each of the times he has seen or imagined them. Every detail of any event is forever etched on his memory: 'He told me: "I alone have more memories than all mankind has probably had since the world has been a world."'[35] This has two major consequences: insomnia and an inability to develop general ideas.

Borges' tale presents Funes' condition as a metaphor for insomnia. Having substituted episodic or autobiographical memory with total recall, stuffed full of details and with no periods of latency, Funes takes exactly the same amount of time to recall his day as he spends experiencing it directly. He remembers all of the dreams he dreams at night and every image that appears during his waking moments, the reason he loses the ability to distinguish between dreams and reality. Consequently, he struggles to sleep and enjoy its distraction from the details of the world, which have become the daily content of his mind.

Furthermore, he can no longer develop general ideas or conceptualize, as he has lost the ability to extract himself from what he immediately observes and records. He remembers both the single words of a discourse and the single letters that make up each word, never able to distract his attention away from the minutiae. In other words, he sacrifices the expressions and significance of general meaning in order to focus on each grammatical element of which they are composed. This inability to think in an abstract way, to generalize or conceptualize due to a total recall that leaves no free space, is a handicap that Funes shares with Solomon Shereshevsky, whose case was studied by Alexandr Romanovic Luria, a twentieth-century Russian psychologist. In his book, *The Mind of a Mnemonist*, Luria describes this man, referred to as S., as having as prodigious a memory as Funes, caused by an unusual synaesthesia. He is able to create immediate associations between words, colours, shapes and images. This carries with it the ability to remember every single minute detail, including seemingly senseless mathematical formulae. However, the visual immediacy of the memories and the instant assimilation of details generates a progressive incapacity to gain a comprehensive view of things. S. limits himself to seeing a series of proposed data and transforming every word or number that he hears into images, without being able to reflect on it in an abstract way, and therefore, conceptualize and comprehend the general sense of meaning, exactly as happens to Funes.[36]

Two reflections found in Borges' short story are worth particular attention. The first involves Funes' awareness that he would reach the moment of his death without having finished classifying even his childhood memories. The second, closely linked to the first, involves the only way in which a memory such as Funes' can be defined: in short, a 'garbage heap'.[37] In other words, the story of Funes seems to agree with what Nietzsche and Canetti believe. Nietzsche imagines a man precisely like Funes, with no ability to forget and who is condemned to see a sense of flux in everything. 'Such a human being', observes the German philosopher, 'would no longer believe in his own being, would no longer believe in himself, would see everything flow apart in turbulent particles, and would lose himself in this stream of becoming.'[38] Canetti peremptorily maintains that this must involve three degrees of despair: 'not remembering anything, remembering something, remembering everything'.[39]

Creating Space in Memory: Forgetting and Sleep as Forms of Resistance

Funes' memory is the literary equivalent of the MyLifeBits project created by Bell and Gemmell with their lifelogging process: a memory that conserves everything and forgets nothing, devoid of empty spaces or interruptions. Funes' experience is much like the memory of a smartphone which, filled with applications, images and data, finds its available space reduced to just a few megabytes. In this case, the user receives an automatic message warning them their phone memory is running out. The message advises them to free up some space, first by eliminating the waste of the caches, the non-fundamental data of applications and all the content (images, videos, rarely used applications, etc.) uses up so many gigabytes. Without drastic action, the phone's applications and various functions stop working properly. There is a significant slowing down: you are no longer notified of new emails, it is no longer possible to store new images or videos, it becomes difficult to load websites. In other words, filling all of the digital memory, reducing the available space with material that is often insignificant or superfluous, means automatically rendering the device inefficient and slowing response times. This blocks the recording of new content and reduces the capacity to manage and reproduce what it already holds. Filling all the space means turning digital memory into a garbage heap, just like Funes' memory after the incident.

The symbolic proximity between Funes' memory and that of a smartphone crammed full of data brings to light the issues intrinsic in any attempt to preserve *presence* over any *absence*, filling all the available space. It is undeniable that absence and lack cause enormous suffering in those subjected to their consequences. Aleida Assmann, with regard to the relationship between remembering and forgetting, demonstrates how the two concepts generally tend to produce well-defined pairs of opposites: the act of remembering is associated with the adjectives good, difficult, costly, slow and conscious, while the act of forgetting has the adjectives bad, easy, free, quick and unconscious.[40] However, the fact that forgetting generates pain, and is therefore historically interpreted in a negative way, does not automatically mean that remembering without forgetting leads to lasting wellbeing. As William James observes, 'If we remembered everything, we should on most occasions be as ill off as if we remembered nothing [...] Without totally forgetting a prodigious number of states of consciousness, and momentarily forgetting a large number, we could not remember at all.'[41] The absence and empty spaces that precede what currently exists provide the conditions necessary for each of us to look to our own futures without feeling held back by the constant presence of spectres from the past. In this regard, Mayer-Schönberger states, 'too perfect a recall, even when it is benignly intended to aid our decision-making, may prompt us to become caught up in our memories, unable to leave our past behind, and much like Borges' Funes, incapable of abstract thoughts'.[42] We will return to this aspect shortly.

For the moment, I would like to focus on three reflections that, starting with the bond between Funes and total digital recall, highlight a number of difficulties inherent in the age of sharing our passions (for more than ten years) on Facebook, Instagram, Twitter and on our own mobile devices.

First is the juxtaposition of a memory without forgetting and a garbage heap, illustrated masterfully by the artworks mentioned in the first chapter: *Suns from Sunsets from Flickr* and *Photography in Abundance*. Both use the artistic tools at their disposal to demonstrate how the compulsive accumulation of photographic images and video-recordings of every lived experience automatically renders them superfluous and useless. The absence of any rational way of archiving those images that immortalize our experiences on a daily basis, in a way that would render them meaningful, means their value is circumscribed to the time during which they are present on social media profiles, and only for as long as their visibility guarantees the highest number of likes. Digital objects live in the moment and according to a timely reaction from others. It is unlikely they are looked at and exhumed a second time, not least because they are immediately submerged and therefore hidden by all those that follow.

There are vague parallels between a suffocating immersion in an ocean of images and the effects of disposophobia, the mental disorder that leads individuals to accumulate an incalculable quantity of useless objects that make all domestic space progressively uninhabitable. Stuffing the internet and our own electronic devices with images and content automatically transforms these objects into a chaotic mass of fragments that, in the long term, lose any connection to the experiences they depict.

This is demonstrated by American scholar Linda Henkel, who coined the eloquent phrase *photo-taking impairment effect*. After a series of experiments conducted for the University of Fairfield (Connecticut) and published in the review *Psychological Science*, Henkel noted an objective correlation between the inability to memorize lived experiences and the uncontrolled accumulation of photographs on personal mobile devices. Henkel asked some thirty students to look at a number of artworks found in a local museum. She subdivided them so that some simply observed dozens of objects, while others were also able to photograph them with their smartphones. Having set them a memory test the next day, she noted how those who had simply observed the objects without photographing them were able to remember more details than the others. More proof that filling all the available space seems to generate the opposite effect of that desired by Bell and Gemmell: autobiographical or episodic memory is not reinforced or improved, but weakened. The use of objective digital memory takes responsibility away from subjective memory, diverting attention away from what is being observed. We might conclude that the pleasure or need to immortalize every experience of one's own life is only useful for constructing one's own autobiographical narrative together with other social network users, and not as a strengthening of one's own personal and exclusive biological memory through a mere accumulation of data on a smartphone. In other words, the compulsive accumulation of photographic images and video-recordings, if it falls within the grand experiment in collective cultural autobiography, proves the full integration of offline and online lives as demonstrated by the TV series SKAM. When, however, it is used to create an objective and mechanical memory understood as a technological antidote to forgetting, it seems to have an entirely inverse effect. As Mark Fisher says, quoting Baudrillard: 'computers don't really remember because they lack the ability to forget'.[43]

Secondly, a memory devoid of forgetting, such as that possessed by Funes, can interfere negatively with certain emotional mechanisms that affect our autobiographical memory. Take the psychological phenomenon known as *flashbulb memories*, whose plausibility is currently the subject of lively international debate. This expression is used to indicate the photographic memories tied to an event that, having featured significantly in the public space, has provoked intense emotional effects both in those who experienced it first hand and those who experienced it indirectly through (for example) newspapers or news programmes. These effects lead to a highly detailed, almost objective recollection of the memory, which also includes a meticulous recall of the details relating to the specific circumstances in which the event took place. In other words, flashbulb memories are photographic memories generated by the trauma associated with a particular experience, which leads to the vivid and detailed recording of the event and the lingering sense of threat and danger. Repeated discussion with relatives, friends and acquaintances then leads to a definitive consolidation of the memory. The most common example used to explain flashbulb memories is that of the 9/11 terror attack in 2001, with particular attention paid to the images and the audiovisual recordings of the collapse of the Twin Towers. Though many scholars are not convinced we can talk about the objective existence of this phenomenon, it makes sense that events capable of combining an elevated level of surprise, intense emotional participation on a collective level and the threat of grave consequences might leave significant and long-lasting impressions on the memory. Objective recording, using a memory without forgetting, could extend indefinitely into the alleged phenomenon of flashbulb memories, making emotional participation in every kind of memory pathologically pervasive.[44] In this way, the dangers imagined in the *Black Mirror* episode *The Entire History of You* would come into effect, in which the possibility of projecting and reproducing one's own memories, objectively recorded by a microchip implanted behind the ear, has the unique effect of pathologically increasing the alienation of a jealous man who suspects his wife is cheating on him.

Thirdly, the juxtaposition of total recall and the insomnia suffered by Funes have a specific pertinence when considered alongside the points made by Jonathan Crary in his book *24/7. Late Capitalism and the Ends of Sleep*. In this text Crary analyses the effects of so-called '24/7 capitalism' in which we find all work activities (supermarkets, call centres, gyms, etc.) carried out without nocturnal pauses or interruptions on holidays or weekends. The author believes the hours of sleep to be the last 'uncompromising interruption of the theft of time from us by capitalism [...] that cannot be colonized and harnessed to a massive engine of profitability'.[45] The scandalous presence of sleep lies in the fact that we are reminded every day, without exception, of the healthy relationship between intermittence and alternation upon which our lives are built: the light of the sun and the dark of the night, daytime activity and nocturnal rest, working hours and leisure time. Sleep 'is an irrational and intolerable affirmation that there might be limits to the compatibility of living beings with the allegedly irresistible forces of modernization'.[46] Today's world, convinced that no natural fact is inalterable, tries in fact to use all technological tools at its disposal to overcome any kind of alternation, which is considered unproductive. Absences and periods of latency are, in other words, a limit to the development of activities that require constant presence and participation.

Crary connects these reflections to both the quest for total recall, as removing any form of forgetting means having your own personal documents to hand at any moment of the day no matter where you are, and to the step that leads from total recall to digital immortality – once death is eliminated, even the final space that had, until now, remained empty and intangible is filled. Both total recall and digital immortality are comparable to non-stop *surveillance* and *recurrence*, which imply always being active and present. The surveillance and recurrence referred to by a world that is brightly lit 24/7 is the ultimate endgame of the hyper-technological capitalist society that demands non-stop productivity and aims to make us inhabit undifferentiated time, demanding peak performance devoid of weakness or empty spaces. It is no surprise, therefore, that Funes suffers from insomnia and is unable to console himself with sleep: 'images have become one of the many depleted and disposable elements that, in their intrinsic archiveability, end up never being discarded'.[47]

The Internet as a Melancholy Container of Regret: Hollie Gazzard, The Last Message Received, Wartherapy

I have so far attempted to demonstrate what the (sometimes dystopian) future might look like in this age of shared passions and daily online construction of one's own autobiographical story, featuring total recall, digital immortality, and multiple insomniac lives without forgetting or death. Now I would like to take a step back and focus on a number of existing consequences of the confusion between data flows and archives. The following examples aim to highlight the complexities involved with the social networks' current metamorphosis into digital archives. On the one hand, the era of shared passions places each of us in the unprecedented position of being able to contribute to a grand experiment in collective cultural autobiography and the creation of encyclopedias of the dead 2.0. In this way, we revolutionize our relationship with writing and self-representation, placing the universal bond between human fragments before single personal demands, while fooling ourselves into thinking that it is possible to remember everything and never die. On the other hand, however, this unique technological era transforms the entirety of online spaces we frequent into a *melancholy container of regret*, which counters digital immortality with the constant reiteration of loss, absence, mourning and, therefore, death itself. Such a situation, complex and contradictory, is the result of our (ongoing) inability to rationally control and manage the ocean of words and images that we produce.

The first example involves a number of unexpected issues caused by the overabundance of memories registered within social networks. The On This Day and Memories sections of Facebook in particular generate situations that are often rather unpleasant (to say the least) for those who accidentally find themselves caught up in them. The parents of Hollie Gazzard, the twenty-year old woman from Gloucester, England who was brutally murdered by her ex-boyfriend while at work on 18 February 2014, know something about this. Hollie, like most of her peers, was very active on social networks, filling her personal profiles on Facebook, Instagram and Twitter with photographic images. Her Facebook account in particular still contains more than a thousand photographic images, which can be viewed by around 700 contacts. After their daughter's murder, the woman's parents found her Facebook profile to be a priceless memory box, as it contained an enormous number of digital footprints left by their daughter. Among the thousands of photographs, however, were 72 that depicted Hollie with her killer, as she had not removed them once the relationship had ended. Some of these images reappear on her wall, automatically exhumed by the On This Day function. This was an event that is highly traumatic for her parents, who are then forced to relive the brutal murder that deprived them of their daughter. The solution to this problem initially seems rather straight forward: the victim's sister had Hollie's log-in details and therefore the possibility of deleting photos once she gained access to her profile. But the moment in which she attempted to access the profile, she realized that it was blocked: the account had become a commemorative profile regardless of the dead woman's wishes as a result of the media frenzy whipped up by the news coverage. Her relatives then asked the powers that be at Facebook to remove these photographs, but they were unsuccessful: the lack of prior authorization by Hollie stops third parties from violating the profile's privacy, which, as we know, is part of her digital identity. It took lengthy court battles and several public campaigns to convince the social network to make an exception and finally delete those photographs.

Gillian Brockell, video editor at the *Washington Post*, experienced a similar situation that she recounted in an open letter sent to Facebook, Twitter, Instagram and Experian, and which went viral throughout the world. In the letter, the woman tells of how she published numerous images on social networks during her pregnancy, adding specific hashtags (#30weekspregnant, #babybump, and so on) to the image captions. She also clicked on several web banners suggested by Facebook advertising maternity wear. After her baby was stillborn, Gillian continued to receive adverts for products relating to newborns and children. The advertising profiling carried out on the basis of information she had previously shared led to the constant proposition of products that should have been of interest to her, but instead made the suffering caused by her loss infinitely more acute. As such, in her letter she asks to no longer see these adverts, pointing out how as well as searching for clothes and objects for newborns, that she also typed into Google phrases such as 'Braxton-Hicks contractions' and 'baby not moving', followed by posts with keywords such as 'broken heart' and 'stillborn', which, however, the algorithms seem to have missed.

These two different cases of Hollie Gazzard and Gillian Brockell highlight both the enormous problems caused by the rigidity of privacy regulations in the presence of painful events such as those described, and users' lack of familiarity with the basic mechanisms of the various Memories and On This Day functions. Facebook, having recognized the negative consequences of 'looking back', have recently created a kind of taxonomy of memory themes which should lead to substantial improvements in the management of shared memories, reducing the occurrence of painful situations for users. This taxonomy consists of a system that selects memories according to specific keywords, from which terms that might be associated with a problematic meaning are excluded. For example, the system excludes digital data that contain the expression 'I miss you', as it reminds us of a

loss. Furthermore, all posts and images in which commemorative profiles of deceased users are tagged are excluded from
On This Day. Following the recent political scandal involving
Cambridge Analytica, Zuckerberg is about to introduce a tool
called Clear History, which will give users the opportunity to
delete their entire chronology from the databases of social
networks. This means users will be able to view the information regarding the applications and websites with which
they have interacted, eliminating it from their Facebook
account. This should limit the use of data collected by third
parties for the creation of targeted advertising, thus avoiding
the repetition of cases such as that of Gillian Brockell.

The second example involves the project named The Last
Message Received (https://thelastmessagereceived.tumblr.
com/), which highlights the substantial limits of the aforementioned taxonomy of memory themes. Created in 2016
by fifteen-year-old Emily Trunko from Ohio, this project
consists of a platform hosted on Tumblr in which screenshots
of the last messages a person has received from someone else
via email, WhatsApp or Messenger are collected, selected
and published. These could be the last message written by:
(a) a partner before the end of a relationship; (b) a friend,
before they literally disappeared (known as ghosting, a term
that indicates someone who metaphorically becomes a ghost
by ceasing to respond to messages, telephone calls or emails
without explanation); and (c) from a relative who dies shortly
after having written and sent the message. The Last Message
Received is, ultimately, a bitter collection of last words, those
that sanction the end of a relationship in a direct or unwanted
way. Trunko's project is similar to The Tweet Hereafter, the
internet site that collects and publishes the last tweets written
by someone who (famous or otherwise) was unable to write
any more due to their death. What differentiates The Last
Message Received from The Tweet Hereafter is, firstly, the
content of these messages which, being private, are more
articulated, intimate and confidential. And secondly, are
the comments that shed light on the messages written by
those who, having received them and agreed to their being
published on the Tumblr-hosted platform, decide to provide
more context in order to facilitate their comprehension.

According to the platform's FAQs (which have not updated since 2016 despite it still being very much active), there are more than 90,000 users interested in reading thousands of last messages. In order to better illustrate the nature of the project, I will discuss a few.

On 2 September 2019, a girl agrees to the publication of the last message received from her friend who committed suicide shortly after sending it: 'It must be wonderful to not remember anything, to be free from memories. I wonder if anyone will remember what I've done.' Underneath the message, the girl leaves a comment in which she wishes her friend, wherever she may be, may never know the pain her actions caused. She adds that she will never forget her, that she misses her, just as every single memory of her brings suffering because she feels guilty for not having been able to stop her suicide. On 25 October 2018, another message displays the affectionate words exchanged between two people before a heroin overdose led to the death of one, as we are informed by the person who decided to share publicly the message's content.

The tone of most of these last words, archived in chronologically descending order, using key words that help us understand the nature of the relationship that has ended, is similar to that of the two messages I have discussed. If we turn our attention away from The Last Message Received to the locations from which these final messages were sent and received, we realize that there is probably no one with a smartphone or computer who doesn't have a conspicuous number of 'last words' among their digital data. They live on eternally in conversations on Messenger, WhatsApp, emails, which we can access 24/7, continually re-reading the written expressions within which a farewell is concealed. Everyone, every day, has at their disposal the primary source of their own personal regret: the final messages before the death of a friend or the end of a relationship, but also all the conversations and images that preceded them. For example, if I want masochistically to revisit the pain of a loss, I can search through my archived messages for those in which a dear friend told me, a few years ago, of a malign tumour that caused his death just two years later. Here, the archive fever described by Derrida emerges in full force, joined by the need to oppose that which disappears, the sense of radical finiteness and the threat of the death drive and urge for destruction. The blackmail by ghosts from a world that has come to an end is almost daily, consisting in the unrelenting repetition of the separation and the body of information that anticipated and prepared us for it. And on top of all that, there are no end of jokes played on us by algorithms: the Facebook notification reminding you to wish a dead person a happy birthday, or from Telegram telling you that the girlfriend that left you or a dead contact (due to their number being reissued after a long period of inactivity) has just joined.

Digital immortality, as an emancipation of the entirety of memories from the person who produced them, is counter-balanced by the infinite reiteration of the loss of the world in its entirety that comes with each death. A trick of fate means that one of the very modalities that allows us to access digital eternity is the repetition of separation and, therefore, regret.

The third and final example involves the experience of Wartherapy, the nickname used by a player of the driving simulation video game, RalliSport Challenge. When he was a child, Wartherapy played against his father all the time, who would always beat him in record time. Simulation videogames like RalliSport Challenge allow you to save and archive top scores and races, preserving them in the game's memory using a 'ghost' function. When his father died, the boy chose not to play RalliSport Challenge for over ten years, finding it too painful a reminder of his loss. One day he decided to open it up again and found himself in a situation he could have never imagined: that of playing against his father's 'ghost'. As the game had saved the times and courses of the top player, his father's car had remained in the race despite the fact the driver had died in offline reality. So, Wartherapy is able to play against his father's ghost, whose car features faded colours and is transparent to show that it is being moved by an automation and not an active player. The curious and moving thing is that the son continued to let his father win. In fact, if the son ever won, the father's car would disappear, unleashing new grief. As such, Wartherapy stops just before the finish line to stop his father dying a second time. Similarly, the reluctance to delete one's own

Facebook account or that, for example, of a dead child is bound to the fear of causing the death of one of our (in the first case) digital identities and, in the second, to repeat the grief endured in the offline dimension.

Retromania and Sad Passions: The End of Nostalgia and the Loss of the Future

Total recall and insomnia, digital immortality and the independence of memories, the internet and regret: reality is increasingly presented to us in the guise of a digital document. Its options are infinite, 'no decision is final, revisions are always possible, and any previous moment can be recalled at any moment'.[48] We know this from our experiences of both the eternal return of final messages, as The Last Message Received teaches us, and the perpetual survival of cancer bloggers through their visual narratives. We can also see this in our constant modification of the digital footprints we produce and leave on social networks, or the moment in which we see the return of people, words and images, that once deleted or simply put to one side, return the same but different each time.

When Schelling talks of the connection between autobiographical writing and the summary of the entire history of the universe, he rigorously separates the present from the past recognized as such, so that the past is understood, the present is known, and the future is foretold and prophetized. In order to do this, he highlights the fundamental role played by nostalgia, which comes about the moment the desire to embrace and exhaust the infinite realizes that it will never be satisfied, because it is impossible to exhaust the infinite. Nostalgia, as such, is not the consequence of a limit imposed by the past, but the awareness that there is no way of placing a limit on the future. Romantic nostalgia implies both a lack of satisfaction, as the desired objective that is never reached, and (careful) a desire to never dissolve this lack of satisfaction, to never reach the desired objective, in the remote eventuality this is even possible. Its constructive nature, fundamental to generating something new and always reaching for a new objective, comes precisely from the constant oscillation between this ambition and the clear awareness that is not advantageous actually to satisfy it.

Reality's identification with a digital document risks compromising this fertile dialectic within nostalgia. The confusion of data flows with archives, the co-existence of the present with a past that seems to have become a world in its own right, as well as the desire to eliminate forgetting and death by filling all the available space, push us to suppose that the future will be nothing but an infinite reiteration of what we have already experienced. The reissuing of what has already happened and the continual disinterment of the body produced by this constant 'looking back' give us reason to suspect that there is insufficient space for creating something new, as everything that exists is filled by marks, footprints, data and information that keep alive a reality that, in their absence, would have inevitably died away. The new, therefore, can no longer present itself as a response to what has been sedimented. Sedimentation, which requires an awareness of the end, has been substituted by presence and reiteration. Nostalgia seems to have reached its ultimate goal, and as such has lost its infinite ambition to search for and (pretend) to conquer it. The epidemic of memory in the online dimension ultimately convinces us that the infinite has finally been embraced and exhausted.

A suffocating sense of heaviness is imposed on nostalgia, which mutates into a form of melancholy that evokes immobilism, regression and a lack of progress. This sense of heaviness is traditionally associated with melancholy. According to the treaty *On the Nature of Man*, which is sometimes attributed to Galen, others to Hippocrates, and others again to his son-in-law Polybus, but was undoubtedly written no later than 400 CE, this is the effect of the three humours (phlegm, yellow bile, and blood) being overwhelmed by black bile, which occurs when it overflows from its base and compromises the isonomy of the whole. Black bile encapsulates everything that stops movement: a dense, sombre substance, usually located in the spleen due to its dark colour, is associated with the autumn as a symbol of maturity (in Ancient times) or advanced age (in the Middle Ages and Renaissance), endowed with the same qualities as earth (cold and dryness) and associated with the planet Saturn. As Aristotle also observes, other characteristics associated with black bile all evoke slowness: a stutter, pale skin, heaviness, laboured movement, anxiety and constant fatigue, surliness and sadness of spirit, arriving at listlessness (Baudelaire's 'heavy foot') and total paralysis.[49] When a sense of heaviness takes over, melancholy leads us to become permanently attached to a past that is not recognized as such, infinitely dilating and extending the present and denying the future any vital enthusiasm. Its final outcome can only be depression, causing a temporal metamorphosis that is even more profound. As Eugenio Borgna writes,

> the dimension of the future (and what is to come) is cut down, severed, amputated, and the present is swallowed up by the past which, with its gigantic sails, aims to reabsorb the present (in order to scatter it), stopping any progress and feeding guilt. The dimension of the past, by amplifying and swelling itself, thus stops the present from spreading into the infinite spaces of time. There is only the past that devours and steals, and there is the epiphany of the past that urges towards a voluntary death as a way of stopping anxiety and suffering in their tracks.[50]

We must recognize that the opportunity to record and preserve an historically unprecedented number of personal memories can transform into the danger of losing that very passion for the future that makes our nostalgia constructive. If we allow ourselves to be overcome by digital memory, we risk being struck down by 'retromania', the incurable pathology discussed by Simon Reynolds and Mark Fisher, which sees us forever ensnared by 'sad passions', which Miguel Benasayag and Gérard Schmit identify as belonging to contemporary society. We run the risk of resigning ourselves to a loss of the future, crushed beneath the weight of a past that remains eternally alive and active and, as such, loses its distinguishing features. Mark Fisher, in agreement with Crary, maintains that modern capitalism aims at making this risk real, as the sense of resignation and impotence, and the lack of future aspiration, reduces all human beings into consumers who hobble on through the ruins.[51]

San Junipero Exists and Lives in Facebook

A perfect artistic representation of the reflections we have just made, which demonstrate the difficulties inherent in managing two different temporalities – online and offline – in a single onlife reality, is offered by San Junipero, the imaginary world described in another episode of *Black Mirror*. San Junipero is the result of a particular nostalgia therapy, used predominantly with tetraplegic patients and those with Alzheimer's disease, which consists of the patient's mental delocalization to the past and its various cultural expressions. This delocalization takes place in a world (San Junipero) where pain does not exist, and which is regulated by the laws of enjoyment and disengagement, in which 'tourists' live alongside digital spectres of the dead. It connects to an idealized past from which all dark corners and negative emotions are eliminated. The future travels backwards through time, relocating itself in a past era devoid of the traumas that occurred later (such as the death of a spouse or a child). San Junipero is, above all, a mental representation of our current way of imagining the 1980s and 1990s. We find ourselves young and healthy inside timeless nightclubs playing *Girlfriend in a Coma* by The Smiths and *Don't You (Forget About Me)* by Simple Minds, *Fake* by Alexander O'Neal and *Heaven is a Place on Earth* by Belinda Carlisle. The choice of songs according to their titles is clearly no coincidence, the perfect description of this greatest hits of memories in which vintage pop fashions and cultures, lifestyles and music find their perfect fit in an eternity styled on Netflix or YouTube. San Junipero is ultimately the depiction of eternity as a mental location in the past, whose inhabitants transform their nostalgia into an idealization that evens out everything they were, placing (for example) Beverly Hills 90210 and Nirvana on the same plane, two realities that, when they were current, had nothing in common. It is also the depiction of the independence of memories with which Bell and Gemmell identify digital immortality.

Such a nostalgic therapy would be welcomed by those facing a serious invalidating illness, such as tetraplegia or Alzheimer's disease. Indeed, in the sphere of Digital Health, there are numerous studies carried out all over the world that attempt to combine neuropharmacology and artificial intelligence in order to create virtual opportunities that make real the mental dislocation imagined by *Black Mirror* with San Junipero.[52] The problem is that San Junipero describes a reality that has become the exact equal of a digital document. More than anything else, it offers a cinematic image of the detachment between progress and continuity that happens each day in places such as YouTube, 'which is more like a jumbled attic than an archive, only laxly framed and annotated'.[53] We age biologically, but we convince ourselves we always remain the same, and have done from the moment social networks led us to delude ourselves each day by believing the cultural experiences we have already had are our present. Again, On This Day: the past is here, in reach, always active and available. In other words, social networks offer us the privileges enjoyed by characters in films or television series (almost) without charge. It doesn't matter that Bridget Fonda is now 55: what counts is that Janet Livermore, the character she played in the film *Singles*, set in Seattle in 1992, will never not be 22. Exactly the same thing happens with Wartherapy when he plays the digital spectre of his father in RalliSport Challenge today. The 'freezing' of his dead father's online activity makes it possible for the son, who is now older than his father ever was, to play him, while the father remains eternally frozen at the age he was the last time he played.

From another perspective, San Junipero's realization within social networks is similar to a collective antero-grade amnesia. It digitally transmits among its users the pathology which keeps intact those memories that precede its appearance, meaning it is impossible to store new information in the long-term memory. A famous example of anterograde amnesia is that of Caitlin, whose story inspired the television series *Caitlin Can't Remember* produced by US television channel Fox8. Due to a cerebral trauma sustained during a cross-country run, the 15-year old girl's memory literally stopped on 12 October 2017, the day of the accident. Every morning when she wakes up, all memory of the previous day is wiped out, leaving her convinced that it is always 12 October 2017. As a result, her parents are forced to explain to her every day that time has passed despite it having been eliminated from her memory.

Mark Fisher and Simon Reynolds relate this kind of digital San Junipero that spreads anterograde amnesia, to the contemporary pop-music scene. When, at the end of the 1980s, my parents gave me The Doors' album of the same name (first released in 1967), I recognized both the timeless beauty of the songs on the album (*Light My Fire, The End, Break on Through*, etc.) and the light years between their sound and that which was popular at the time. Their bombastic style (with the Hammond organ in the foreground), the style of recording, the music, were all very dated when compared to the sounds considered fashionable in the late 1980s, whose styles and innovative tendencies were particularly varied: from romantic new wave in the style of Duran Duran, to the dark version offered by The Cure, from Judas Priest's heavy metal to the saxophone-heavy pop of Simply Red. In 2019, when one listens to an album from the 1990s – a great example is *Dirt* by Alice in Chains – the temporal distance is not evident. Fisher even reiterates how, if we were able to travel back in time and give a 1990s music fan the chance to hear a modern rock, pop or techno track, it would cause them no 'future shock' nor any other kind of upset of the kind that formed the basis for the clear distinction between The Doors and Nirvana. 'The high existential angst of Nirvana and Cobain belongs to an older moment; what succeeded them was a pastiche-rock which reproduced the forms of the past without anxiety.'[54] This is due to the ease with which we can find and listen to music today from the past, unlike in other periods in history when, possessing neither YouTube nor the desired album, people relied on it being played spontaneously on radio or television. Reynolds concludes that 'On the internet, the past and present commingle in a way that makes time itself mushy and spongiform. YouTube is quintessentially Web 2.0 in the way that it promises immortality to every video uploaded: theoretically the content could stay up there for ever. You can flit from the archaic to the up-to-the-minute in a click.'[55]

This example of the contemporary use of music highlights how a situation that most people have experienced has changed. It happens to each of us that when we repeatedly go back to a place we associate with a particularly intense memory, whether positive or negative, the emotional impact felt the first time slowly deadens. What follows is the slow and healthy introduction of this place into our present life. The initial memory that we associate with it does not disappear but it becomes less invasive, giving us the possibility to remove it from the reality of the past. The same thing happens when we listen over and over to a song that we haven't heard in a long time, and to which we connect a specific lived experience. The reiteration of the present in its melody helps us understand that the past is just a simulation in our minds, a story we tell ourselves. If we trample over it, enough it is destroyed, still leaving a trace of itself within us but liberating the place and the song from the weight with which we had suffocated it.[56] For example, in a case such as that of Desmond Morris, an alternative to the erasure of all memories would have been a momentary detachment from the places that keep the deceased alive, before then progressively reintroducing them into the present once what happened after their death has been definitively separated from what came before. The San Junipero effect produced by social networks reiterates experiences, yes, but it does not separate them from the past. If anything, it binds them to the impossibility of producing new memories, meaning we relive them as if today were still yesterday.

These final reflections, which bring to light the issues that derive from the metamorphosis of social networks into digital archives, do not aim to be negative in their consideration of the era of shared passions, which, as we have seen in this book, offers many brand-new opportunities for narrative and, as such, personal memory. Rather, they aim to offer pause for thought to new generations in particular who, because of when they were born, are beginning to record, share and accumulate their own digital data. Namely, why we should focus on the instant nature of digital data, leaving the past where it is and protect forgetting from attacks by those who, plagued by insomnia, are always alert. Ultimately, the experience of those who have been subjected to the epidemic of memory offers an opportunity to avoid making the same mistakes.

Conclusion

Digital Inheritance and a Return to Oblivion

Digital Inheritance: What to Do With Our Own Memories?

Experiments in collective cultural autobiography, encyclopedias of the dead, epidemics of memory, the refusal of the past and the loss of the future. The complex and, at times, inextricable link that we have with our memories leads us, by way of conclusion, to ask ourselves what we can actually do to manage our memory in the age of the social network.

First, we must quickly put our superstitions to one side, and accept that which we are constantly repressing in our daily lives, aided by the lack of preparation shown by the society in which we live: death is a certainty, its arrival cannot be planned in advance and there is no contract that guarantees being able to live to old age. It is possible that before we die (a case of luck rather than certainty) debilitating illnesses such as Alzheimer's disease, senile dementia and any other pathology that snatches away lucidity and our ability to take decisions autonomously, may impede the use of our own decisional power. To this certainty that our lives will end and the possibility of a debilitating disease, we can add our awareness, highlighted many times over in this book, that biological death does not mean digital death. The

Grim Reaper is only interested in the individual's psycho-physical presence, not their multiple digital presences spread throughout the internet. He is, in other words, entirely indifferent to the activities developed and managed by his victim in the online dimension before his unexpected arrival.

Having taken this on board, it is worth organizing a digital will in advance, as well as a biological one. The legal framework regarding digital inheritance is still somewhat vague. In Italy, for example, there is no specific legislation on the matter. The absence of any legislative support means we have to face, perhaps with the help of a solicitor, the reality of creating an inventory of the multiple informational souls we have left throughout the online world. Social networks, email inboxes, blogs, home banking, dating sites, books and musical playlists, online shopping services, and Netflix, not to mention all those places in which personal memories are held (Cloud Storage, computers, tablets, smartphones, USB drives, external memory drives, etc.). This task may seem arduous, an exhaustive inventory is probably impossible, but tangible steps can be taken.

First: everyone must write down, either on a piece of paper or on a printed document, the login details for the online places they regularly visit. If passwords have changed over the years, these details will need to be updated. Once this has been done, you must choose: which informational souls do you want to consign to oblivion? Which, instead, do you want to live on after your death? And how should they be kept alive: wandering autonomously and anarchically through the online locations that host them or managed by a trusted heir (with what is known as a post-mortem mandate)?

Second: everyone must discuss this creation of the aforementioned inventory openly with their loved ones. Almost all the people who have mourned a death and with whom I have interacted since the publication of my book *Online Afterlives*, have confessed to me that the deceased's profiles on social networks, when left active, have proven both a treasured place of memory as they contain an exorbitant quantity of the footprints left during their lives, and an impediment to mourning in a healthy way (think of the Hollie Gazzard case). Because of the temporal mechanism that characterizes digital technology, all of these footprints keep the deceased alive, making any acceptance of their absence and separation more difficult. For these reasons, a timely discussion with our loved ones helps us find solutions together that cause the least pain to the least amount of people, avoiding needless and excessive arguments between those who would prefer to delete the social media profiles and those who would prefer to keep them active, once death or a debilitating disease has struck.

Third: everyone must familiarize themselves with the services they use so that they are able to take informed decisions together with their loved ones. For example, it is necessary to know the various regulations governing social networks and email inboxes in the event of the account owner's death. It is then important to remember that the headquarters for many of these services is not in our country of residence, so necessary precautions must be taken ahead of time to avoid costly wrangles between relatives and spouses, and international subjects in order to recover the personal data of a loved one who has died prematurely. Again, it is important to remember that some legal rulings have ordered that the heirs of the deceased be given their online data, even in cases in which the online services used guarantee the user that, in the case of their death, their digital objects will be destroyed. For example, in 2018, after five years of legal battles, a German court ruled in favour of a request by the parents of a teenage girl who had tragically died, to access her Facebook profile in an attempt to understand why it had happened. All despite the rules governing Facebook, which guarantee absolute protection of the privacy of every single user. The court found that the heirs' right must prevail over the privacy of the deceased and her contacts, with whom she may have interacted privately. Ultimately, knowing that even one's own children cannot plan their own death, it is important to know the online locations they frequent. How many parents, for instance, know that TikTok exists and that it is the online location most frequented by their children today? How many are aware of the accounts their children open on YouTube, often hidden behind nicknames, or on other less well-known social networking sites? And in the unfortunate event of their death, what should be done with their telephone numbers, each associated with WhatsApp and Telegram accounts? While deleting the number is equivalent to eliminating a precious source of memories, preserving it means recognizing that, with the passing of time and the inevitable years of inactivity, the number will be reassigned to another user. This is what happened to Chastity Patterson, an American girl who for years wrote symbolic messages to her dead father on WhatsApp, not knowing that they were actually being read by a total stranger who had been assigned her dead father's number. That was until the man revealed himself, responding to her and letting her know that those messages were dear to him, having suffered a similar loss himself. For those who do not want to take that risk, you could ask to inherit the management of the dying relative's telephone number, but this removes the possibility for other people close to them to do what Chastity did, as they will know they are writing to the relative of their dead friend.

Fourth: everyone needs to bear in mind how the more sensitive cases work, such as the management of home banking and, therefore, online current accounts. It is necessary to be aware that if you leave your online access details to your personal account, that person does not automatically inherit the account in the case of your death. An online account is the extension of the offline one in the virtual dimension. Therefore, for an unmarried couple with no children, the closest relatives of the deceased (parents, siblings) are able to freeze the online account in the absence of a will, even if you have given your password to your partner.

Finally: everyone must know that there are specialized services that can attempt to violate the password protection on smartphones, computers, tablets and USB drives, in order to access the deceased's memories. But these services are very often highly expensive. One alternative are the online services such as Deathswitch and My Last Email, that aim to deliver passwords to previously indicated individuals. However, their working life is very brief, so it is necessary to regularly monitor them to check whether or not they are still active.

The Value of Oblivion and the Joy of Being Forgotten

A final, philosophical reflection must be added to the chaotic aspects of digital inheritance. Let's try and reconsider the choice made by Desmond Morris in light of the imposition of the era of shared passions on social networks. On the one hand, we have the need to cancel out all traces in order to limit the pain unleashed by the death of a loved one, while on the other we have our personal urgency to record and accumulate proof of our own existence on a daily basis, in order to protect ourselves from the terror of disappearing forever. It is, therefore, necessary to ask ourselves the most difficult of questions: do we really need to be remembered forever through our digital objects, running the risk of a past with no end? Might it be desirable to instead be forgotten, to attempt to eliminate every trace of ourselves left over the course of our lives, and therefore to sacrifice our memories in the name of a healthy rediscovery of the future?

We can answer this question with the words used by W.G. Sebald to reflect on funeral rites during a trip to Corsica. Aware that the number of people living on the planet would triple in the near future, and that there was no longer any reason to fear the population of the dead that was once so very powerful, he maintains that 'the dead must now be cleared out of the way as quickly and comprehensively as possible'. He notes how in contemporary metropolises, every individual can be replaced from one moment to the next, and has probably has been redundant since birth:

> For a while the site called the Memorial Grove recently set up on the internet may endure; here you can lay those particularly close to you to rest electronically and visit them. But this virtual cemetery too will dissolve into the ether, and the whole past will flow into a formless, indistinct silent mass. And leaving a present without memory, in the face of a future that no individual mind can envisage, in the end we shall ourselves relinquish life without feeling any need to linger at least for a while, nor shall we be impelled to pay return visits from time to time.[1]

Sebald's thoughts include reflections by Vladimir Jankélévitch, who compares the *oblivion* that 'erodes and flattens all misfortune, consoles all despair, reabsorbs every tragedy along its path', with the *regret* left by the deaths of others, which 'inevitably end up being erased in the heart of eternity'. He concludes that the death that has generated the regret 'will soon count no more than the death of passer-by killed by a falling rock in Taranto two thousand years ago'.[2]

Social networks, by separating regret from oblivion, try in all possible ways to oppose the idea that sooner or later we will all disappear, by utilizing the proliferation of multiple digital I's from a single psycho-physical presence. On the one hand, they aim to create the encyclopedia of the dead imagined by Danilo Kiš, jealously guarding tens of thousands of personal memories that the deceased has recorded within it over the course of their lives. On the other, they consciously transform the extension of the unique psycho-physical presence represented by the digital identities into a genuine technological substitution of the same, as if these identities were able to live on autonomously in our absence. Exactly as happens with San Junipero through the mental dislocation of the ill.

Despite all this effort, social networks can do nothing to protect us from the risk, present in every moment, of disappearing into the ether like the virtual cemetery Sebald spoke of. This is demonstrated by the majority of online places, described in the first part of this book, that have completely disappeared together with all the content accumulated within them over the years. Splunge, Kronic, Vermario.com, MusicbOOm, SixDegrees.com, just like the conversations I held over email between 2000 and 2006, have disappeared from the internet along with millions of public and private pages, leaving nothing but a few incomplete traces within the Internet Archive. Indeed, during Spring 2019, the world was shocked by news of the loss of fifty million songs shared on MySpace between 2013 and 2015, due to a problem with server migration. The destiny of social networks and every other online location do not, therefore, look that different from that of offline meeting places which, having left their mark on a city over the years, then close down. Minuscule traces of these places remain only in the memories of those who frequented them in person and of those who had heard stories linked to their existence; traces that will disappear entirely the day the last person who remembers it dies. This is a destiny shared with every single individual, as we are taught by Pixar's animated film *Coco*, when it reminds us that the eternal memory or oblivion of a dead person's spirit depends on a single photograph.

Such obviously trivial considerations should give us cause to reflect upon the meaning we attribute to the posts we share on social networks and the eventual achievement of digital immortality through the emancipation of digital memories from those who produced them. Any technological transformation over the course of years to come could, in one stroke, eliminate the epidemic of memory that plagues today's era, consolidating our atavistic fear of disappearing. As such, it is necessary calmly to connect the awareness that nothing can stop our total disappearance from the face of this Earth with a careful use of the opportunities offered by digital technology. The importance taken on by the thoughts, words, images and videos of our lives is wholly fleeting. So why not simply enjoy the benefits of our onlife here, in the present? Borges, when discussing Funes' memory, admits never dwelling on his own memories. Instead he turns his gaze to the future, so as to avoid the suffocating burden of the past, the outcome of which is to transform memory into pathological insomnia. Such an attitude could act as a starting point from which to use social networks, focusing our own attention on live streaming, as happens with Stories, or on the immediate validation obtained by what we share. From another perspective, we can have fun with the extensions of our own psycho-physical presence, making it multiple, incoherent, indecipherable and fantastical in order to broaden our horizons and avoid generating epidemics of memories that exhaust constructive nostalgia. In this way, despite the melancholy traps that accompany the act of recording, we can minimize the value attributed to our digital spectres by recognizing that forgetting reminds us that we are mortal, and that appearing and disappearing are two integral parts of the same symbolic concatenation.

In other words, a scrupulous and widespread Death Education, combined with a rational management of our multiple digital I's, can bring about a significant improvement in the way in which we use social networks with regard to memory and oblivion. And, perhaps, it can truly allow every fragment of the interconnected global mind to broaden the surrealist vision of a dream culture in the here and now, before it vanishes into the ether, finally causing our own autobiographical writing to coincide momentarily with the summary of the history of the entire universe.

That said, a day will come in which someone will accidentally find this book, whose form as a hard copy (ironically) will preserve it from oblivion much more effectively than its digital version. They will turn their attention to reflections on places that have entirely disappeared, and they will ask themselves whether the author is describing a reality that truly existed or simply giving free rein to his own hallucinations. And it is right that this is the case.

Notes

Introduction. Social Networks and Looking Back

1 Jonathan Gottschall, *The Storytelling Animal: How Stories Make Us Human*, Houghton Mifflin Harcourt, New York 2012, p. 169.
2 Aleida Assmann, *Sette modi di dimenticare* [*Seven Ways of Forgetting*], Il Mulino, Bologna 2019, p. 23.
3 Antonella Tarpino, *Geografie della memoria. Case, rovine, oggetti quotidiani*, [*Geographies of Memory. Houses, Ruins, Daily Objects*] Einaudi, Turin 2008, p. 27.
4 Umberto Eco, *La memoria vegetale e altri scritti di bibliofilia* [*The Vegetal Memory and Other Writings on Bibliophilia*], La Nave di Teseo, Milan 2018, pp. 9–10.
5 Thomas Hobbes, *De corpore*, in *Human Nature and De Corpore Politico*, ed. J.C.A. Gaskin, Oxford University Press 2008, p. 220: 'In memory, the phantasms we consider are as they were if worn out by time; but in our fancy we consider them as they are [...] The perpetual arising of phantasms, both in sense and imagination, is that which we commonly call discourse of the mind, and is common to with other living creations. For he that thinketh notice of their likeness or unlikeness to one another.'
6 Bertolt Brecht, *In Praise of Forgetting*, in *The Collected Poems of Bertolt Brecht*, trans. and ed. David Constantine and Tom Kuhn, W.W. Norton and Company, London 2018, p. 646.

7 Walter Benjamin, 'Paris, Capital of the Nineteenth Century', in *Reflections*, trans. Edmund Jephcott, Schocken Books, New York 1986, pp. 155–6.
8 Kevin Kelly, *The Inevitable. Understanding the 12 Technological Forces That Will Shape Our Future*, Penguin, New York 2017, p. 61.
9 See Elias Canetti, *Il libro contro la morte* [*The Book Against Death*], Adelphi, Milan 2017, p. 49. For the German original, *Das Buch gegen den Tod*, Hanser Literaturverlage.
10 Within the concept of *Digital Death* we find the various ways in which digital technology is changing our connection to death, mourning and immortality. For more on this, see my book *Online Afterlives. Immortality, Memory and Grief in Digital Culture*, MIT Press 2020.
11 Elaine Kasket, *All the Ghosts in the Machine. Illusions of Immortality in the Digital Age*, Robinson, London 2019.
12 Kenneth Goldsmith, *Wasting Time on the Internet*, HarperCollins, New York 2016, p. 99.
13 Aleida Assmann, *Sette modi di dimenticare* [*Seven Ways of Forgetting*], op. cit., p. 52.
14 Vilem Flusser, *Kommunikologie weiter denken. Die Bochumer Vorlesungen*, Fisher Verlag, Frankfurt am Main 1998, p. 251. See also Byung-Chul Han, *The Expulsion of the Other: Society, Perception and Communication Today*, trans. Wieland Hoban, Polity, Cambridge 2018, p. 5.
15 J.J. Bachofen, *Lebensrückschau*, in H.G. Kippenberg (ed.), *Mutterrecht und Urreligion*, Stuttgart 1984, p. 11.
16 Roland Barthes, *Camera Lucida. Reflections on Photography*, trans. Richard Howard, Hill and Wang, New York 1981, p. 84.
17 Mark Fisher, *Ghosts of My Life. Writings on Depression, Hauntology and Lost Futures*, Zero Books 2014, p. 2.

1 From Social Networks to Digital Archives

1 For more on the three conjoined actions that define social networks, see in particular D. Boyd, N.B. Ellison, 'Social Network Sites: Definition, History, and Scholarship' in *Journal of Computer-Mediated Communication*, 13 (1), 2007, pp. 210–30. For more on the new rules for individuals in the public space, see. L. Paccagnella, A. Vellar, *Vivere online. Identità, relazioni, conoscenza* [*Living Online. Identity, Relations, Knowledge*], Il Mulino, Bologna 2016, in particular pp. 19 ff.
2 See Éric Sadin, *La siliconizzazione del mondo. L'irresistibile*

espansione del liberismo digitale [*The Siliconization of the World. The Irresistible Expansion of Digital Liberalism*] Einaudi, Turin 2018, pp. 141 ff. Originally published in French, *La silicolonisation du monde: L'irrésistible expansion du libéralisme numérique*, Éditions L'Échappée 2016.

3 Giorgio De Maria, *The Twenty Days of Turin: A Novel*, trans. Roland Glazov, Liveright, New York 2017, p. 59, epUB.

4 Ibid., p. 60.

5 Ibid., p. 62.

6 Ibid., p. 63.

7 Ibid., p. 75.

8 Ibid., p. 64. See also Jaron Lanier, *Ten Arguments for Deleting Your Social Media Accounts Right Now*, Vintage 2019, p. 63 epUB.

9 Giorgio De Maria, *The Twenty Days of Turin: A Novel*, op. cit., p. 76.

10 Tatiana Bazzichelli, *Networking. The Net as Artwork*, Digital Aesthetics Research Centre, Aarhus University, 2008, p. 77.

11 See Luciano Floridi, *L'estensione dell'intelligenza: guida all'informatica per filosofi* [*The Extension of Intelligence: A Philosopher's Guide to Information Technology*, Armando, Rome 1996, p. 97.

12 Joan Fontcuberta, *La furia delle immagini. Note sulla postfotografia* [*The Fury of Images. Notes on Post-Photography*, Einaudi, Turin 2018, pp. 14–15. Fontcuberta's observation is actually slightly imprecise. A year previously, in 1996, instant visual communication was already active, thanks to JenniCAM, the site that transmits the life of Jennifer Ringley for 24 hours a day. The twenty-year-old student had installed a webcam in her room at Dickinson College, Pennysylvania, to record and broadcast online everything she did on a daily basis, including her sexual activity. JenniCAM was active from 1996 to 2003. The scholar Krissi M. Jimroglou, in an essay from 1999, describes Ringley's experiment as the birth of a cyborg subjectivity that hybridizes the actual physical presence with technology through the use of the internet. See Krissi M. Jimroglou, 'A Camera with a View: JenniCAM, Visual Representation, and Cyborg Subjectivity', *Information, Communication and Society*, 2 (4), 1999, 439–53.

13 Fabio Santolini, *Sei gradi di separazione telematica* [*Six Degrees of Telematic Separation*], *La Repubblica*, 7 December 1998. https://www.repubblica.it/online/sessi_stili/seigradi/seigradi/seigradi.html.

14 Michael S. Malone, *The Guardian of All Things: The Epic Story of Human Memory*, St Martin's Press, New York 2012, p. 242.

15 Alessandro Baricco, *The Game*, Einaudi, Turin 2018, p. 122.

16 Stefano Quintarelli, *Capitalismo immateriale. Le tecnologie digitali e il nuovo conflitto sociale* [*Immaterial Capitalism. Digital Technologies and the New Social Conflict*], Bollati Boringhieri, Turin 2019, pp. 21 ff.; F. Berardi (Bifo), *After the Future*, AK Press, Chico CA 2011, p. 68, epUB.

17 See Robert Pepperell, *The Posthuman Condition: Consciousness Beyond the Brain*, University of Chicago Press, Chicago IL 1995, in particular pp. 171–2 and p. 177.

18 Pierre Lévy, *Becoming Virtual. Reality in the Digital Age*, Perseus Books, New York 1998, pp. 43–4.

19 Antonio Caronia, 'Corpi e informazioni. Il post-human da Wiener a Gibson' [*Bodies and Information. The Post-human from Wiener to Gibson*], in M. Pireddu, A. Tursi (ed.), *Post-umano. Relazioni tra uomo e tecnologia nella società delle reti* [*Post-Human. Relationships Between Humankind and Technology*], Guerini e associati, Milan 2006, p. 47.

20 Francesca Alfano Miglietti, *Identità mutanti. Dalla piega alla piaga: esseri delle contaminazioni contemporanee* [*Mutant Identities: Beings of Contemporary Contaminations*], Mondadori, Milan 2004, p. 66.

21 See also Silvia Martinelli, *Diritto all'oblio e motori di ricerca. Memoria e privacy nell'era digitale* [*The Right to Oblivion and Search Engines*], Giuffré, Milan 2017, p. 44.

22 William Gibson, *Neuromancer*, Gateway 2016, p. 5.

23 Michele De Russi, 'Computer, cocaina del futuro' [Computers. The Cocaine of the Future], in *La Stampa*, 25 January 1990. I would like to thank Nunzio Fiore, one of my Facebook 'friends', for having publicly shared the photograph of this article on his profile page on 20 October 2019.

24 These two possible relationships to humanity's adjustment to new technology are theorized by philosopher Günther Anders in the 1950s in reference to the effects of the technological and industrial revolutions that occurred over the XIX and XX centuries. See Günther Anders, *L'uomo è antiquato. I. Considerazioni sull'anima nell'epoca della seconda rivoluzione industriale* [*The Outdatedness of Human Beings 1. On the Soul in the Era of the Second Industrial Revolution*], Bollati Boringhieri, Turin 2007. Originally published in German as *Die Antiquiertheit des Menschen Bd 1: Über die Seele im Zeitalter der zweiten industriellen Revolution*.

25 Stefano Boni, *Homo comfort. Il superamento tecnologico della*

fatica e le sue conseguenze [*Homo Comfort. Technology's Defeat of Hard Work, and its Consequences*] Elèuthera, Milan 2014, p. 98.

26 Sherry Turkle, *Alone Together. Why We Expect More from Technology and Less from Each Other*, Basic Books, New York 2011, p. 12.

27 See the article *Facebook sbanca in Italia+ 2.700% di utenti nel 2008* [*Facebook Cleans Up in Italy: +2,700% more users in 2008*], published in Italian newspaper *La Stampa* on 16 April 2009. https://www.lastampa.it/tecnologia/2009/04/16/news/facebook-sbanca-in-italia-2-700-di-utenti-nel-2008-1.37067115.

28 Jay David Bolter and Richard Grusin, *Remediation: Understanding New Media*, MIT Press 2000, p. 243.

29 W.G. Sebald, *Austerlitz*, Penguin Essentials, London 2001, p. 31.

30 Kenneth Goldsmith, *Wasting Time on the Internet*, op. cit., p. 60.

31 See Giuseppe Riva, *Selfie. Narcisismo e identità* [*Selfie. Narcissism and Identity*], Il Mulino, Bologna 2016, pp. 96–7.

32 Simon Reynolds, *Retromania. A Pop Culture's Addiction to Its Own Past*, Faber and Faber, London 2011, p. 56.

33 Joan Fontcuberta, *La furia delle immagini* [*The Fury of Images*], op. cit., p. 27.

34 Ibid., p. 21.

35 All data relating to the number of shared posts, which take place every sixty seconds on the different social networks, are taken from the infographic that collates the research carried out in 2019 by Domo, a company that produces an integrated data management platform. See https://www.domo.com/learn/data-never-sleeps-7.

36 Kevin Kelly, *The Inevitable*, p. 165.

37 Ibid., p. 20.

38 Luciano Floridi, *The Fourth Revolution. How the Infosphere is Reshaping Human Reality*, Oxford University Press 2014, p. 13. Floridi states that 'one exabyte corresponds to 10^{18} bytes or a 50,000 year-long video of DVD quality' (note 5, p. 236).

39 Yuval Noah Harari, *Homo Deus. A Brief History of Tomorrow*, Random House, London 2016, pp. 386–90.

40 Kenneth Goldsmith, *Wasting Time on the Internet*, op. cit., p. 52.

41 Floridi, *The Fourth Revolution*, p. 106.

42 Ed Finn, *What Algorithms Want. Imagination in the Age of Computing*, MIT Press 2018, pp. 76–7. See also Franco Berardi

(Bifo), *Futurability. The Age of Impotence and the Horizon of Possibility*, Verso, London 2019, pp. 209–10.

43 Francesco Paolo De Ceglia, 'Aldilà digitale. Come internet ha cambiato il nostro rapporto con la morte' [The Digital Hereafter. How the Internet has Changed our Relationship with Death], in *Il Tascabile*, 30 August 2018. https://www.iltascabile.com/societa/morte-social/.

44 James Bridle, *New Dark Age. Technology and the End of Future*, Verso, London 2019, pp. 10–11.

45 Douglas Rushkoff, *Present Shock. When Everything Happens Now*, Penguin, New York 2013, p. 85.

2 Collective Cultural Autobiographies and Encyclopedias of the Dead 2.0

1 Kenneth Goldsmith, *Wasting Time on the Internet*, op. cit., p. 80.

2 Tomás Maldonado, *Memoria e conoscenza. Sulle sorti del sapere nella prospettiva digitale* [Memory and Knowledge. On the Fate of Knowledge in Digital Perspective], Feltrinelli, Milan 2005, p. 30.

3 Giorgio De Maria, *The Twenty Days of Turin*, p. 63.

4 Franco Berardi (Bifo), *Futurability*, op. cit., p. 210.

5 Kenneth Goldsmith, *Uncreative Writing. Managing Language in the Digital Age*, Columbia University Press, New York 2011, p. 15.

6 Kevin Kelly, *The Inevitable*, op. cit., p. 104.

7 F.W.J. Schelling, *The Ages of the World*, SUNY, New York 2000, p. 3.

8 The description of human beings as existing in a 'living rotation' can be found in F.W.J. Schelling, *Clara*, SUNY, New York 2002, p. 37. Their description as an 'eternal article' can instead be found in F.W.J. Schelling, *System of Transcendental Idealism (1800)*, University of Virginia Press, 1993, p. 203.

9 F.W.J. Schelling, 'Aforismi introduttivi alla filosofia della natura', in *Aforismi sulla filosofia della natura* ['Introductory Aphorisms to the Philosophy of Nature' in Aphorisms on the Philosophy of Nature], eds. G. Moretti and L. Rustichelli, Egea, Milan 1992, p. 65. Originally published in German as *Aphorismen über die Naturfilosophie*, Felix Meiner Verlag, Hamburg 2018.

10 Byung-Chul Han, *Psychopolitics: Neoliberalism and New Technologies of Power*, Verso, London 2017, p. 59.

11 Byung-Chul Han, *The Expulsion of the Other*, p. 3.

12 Ibid., p. 25.
13 Ibid., p. 7.
14 See Sherry. Turkle, *Reclaiming Conversation: The Power of Talk in a Digital Age*, Penguin, New York 2015, pp. 3–58. See also Manfred Spitzer, *Connessi e isolati. Un'epidemia silenziosa*, [*Connected Yet Isolated. A Silent Epidemic*] trans. C. Tatasciore, Corbaccio, Milan 2018, pp. 103 ff.
15 See C.J. Sofka, Social Support 'Internetworks', Caskets for Sale, and More: Thanatology and the Information Superhighway, in *Death Studies*, 21, 1997, Issue 6, pp. 553–74; M. Massimi, A. Charise, *Dying, Death and Mortality: Towards Thanatosensitivity in HCI*, CHI 2009, 4–9 April 2009, Boston, MA.
16 Kenneth Goldsmith, *Uncreative Writing*, p. 34.
17 See Marina Sozzi, *Non sono il mio tumore. Curarsi il cancro in Italia* [*I Am Not My Tumour. Being Treated for Cancer in Italy*], Chiarelettere, Milan 2019, pp. 163 ff.
18 Atul Gawande, *Being Mortal. Medicine and What Matters in the End*, Profile Books, London 2015, p. 77.
19 Virginia Woolf, *On Being Ill*, The Hogarth Press, 1930, p. 32.
20 Max Horkheimer, Theodor W. Adorno, *Dialectic of Enlightenment*, Verso, London 1997, pp. 194–5.
21 For reference, see the following article on cancer bloggers: https://www.marieclaire.com/culture/a19183515/chronically-ill-youtube-stars/.
22 Salvatore Iaconesi, Oriana Persico, *La Cura* [*The Cure*], Codice, Turin 2016, p. 127.
23 Ibid., p. 159.
24 Danilo Kiš, *Encyclopedia of the Dead*, Northwestern University Press, Evanston IL 1997, p. 41.
25 Ibid., pp. 56–7.
26 Aleida Assmann, *Cultural Memory and Western Civilization: Functions, Media, Archives*. Cambridge University Press, Cambridge 2013, p. 385.
27 Danilo Kiš, *Encyclopedia of the Dead*, p. 44.
28 Ibid., p. 64.
29 For a detailed explanation of MyDeathSpace as a collection of digital biographies of the dead, I refer to my book, *Online Afterlives*, op. cit., pp. 79 ff.
30 Aleida Assmann, *Cultural Memory and Western Civilization*, p. 19.
31 Robin M. Kovalsky, A. McCord, 'If I Knew Then What I Know Now: Advice to My Younger Self', *Journal of Social*

Psychology, 5 May 2019. https://www.tandfonline.com/doi/full/10.1080/00224545.2019.1609401

32 Aleida Assmann, *Sette modi di dimenticare* [*Seven Ways of Forgetting*], op. cit., p. 15 [my italics].

33 See P. Bekinschtein, N.V. Weisstaub, F. Gallo, M. Renner and M.C. Anderson, 'A Retrieval-Specific Mechanism of Adaptive Forgetting in the Mammalian Brain', *Nature Communications*, 9 (2018). https://www.nature.com/articles/s41467-018-07128-7.

34 Frederic C. Bartlett, *Remembering: A Study in Experimental and Social Psychology*, Cambridge University Press, Cambridge 1932.

35 Jan Assmann, *Cultural Memory and Early Civilization. Writing, Remembrance, and Political Imagination*, Cambridge University Press, New York 2012, p. 17.

36 Italo Svevo, *Death*, in *Short Sentimental Journey, and Other Stories*, University of California Press 1967, p. 302.

37 Jonathan Gottschall, *The Storytelling Animal: How Stories Make Us Human*, p. 161. As for the example referencing Goethe's autobiography, see J.W. von Goethe, *Truth and Poetry*, Cambridge University Press, Cambridge 2013.

38 Jean Baudrillard, *Symbolic Exchange and Death*, SAGE, Newbury Park CA 2016, p. 180.

39 Kenneth Goldsmith, *Uncreative Writing*, p. 176.

40 Already at the end of the 1990s there were many studies dealing with the internet's unique temporality. I would recommend in particular: J. Gleick, *Faster: The Acceleration of Just About Everything*, Little Brown and Company, London 1999, pp. 254 ff. See also E. Grosz, *Becomings: Explorations in Time, Memory, and Futures*, Cornell University Press, Ithaca 1999, pp. 59 ff.

41 Douglas Rushkoff, *Present Shock*, op. cit., p. 115.

42 Ibid., p. 115.

43 Ibid., p. 10.

3 Total Recall, Digital Immortality, Retromania

1 Gordon Bell and Jim Gemmell, *Total Recall. How the E-Memory Revolution Will Change Everything*, E.P. Dutton and Co. Boston MA, 2009, p. 93.

2 Ibid., p. 140

3 Ibid., p. 140.

4 Ibid., p. 140. See also Guy Brown, *The Living End: The Future*

of *Death, Aging and Immortality*, Macmillan Science 2007, pp. 115–32.

5 Gordon Bell and Jim Gemmell, *Total Recall. How the E-Memory Revolution Will Change Everything*, p. 151.

6 Kenneth Goldsmith, *Wasting Time on the Internet*, op. cit., p. 97 in English version.

7 Gordon Bell and Jim Gemmell, *Total Recall. How the E-Memory Revolution Will Change Everything*, pp. 38–9

8 Ibid., p. 88.

9 Anna Reading, 'Memobilia: The Mobile Phone and the Emergence of Wearable Memories', in Joanne Garde-Hansen, Andrew Hoskins, Anna Reading (eds), *Save As ... Digital Memories*, Palgrave Macmillan, New York 2009, p. 82.

10 Kevin Kelly, *The Inevitable*, p. 206.

11 Ibid., p. 207.

12 On this subject I would recommend the fascinating article by A.D. Signorelli, '*Un giorno potremo 'proiettare' i sogni come fossero film?*' [*Will We One Day Be Able To 'Project' Our Dreams As If They Were Films?*], in *Wired*, 26 October 2019. https://www.wired.it/attualita/tech/2019/10/26/riprodurre-sogni-come-film/?fbclid=IwAR0HjZFsVxiwbU-AvON2fwsCb Le0jTJmOBfoVYet91pdDXDwOn6ce1m7138.

13 See Gordon Bell and Jim Gemmell, *Total Recall. How the E-Memory Revolution Will Change Everything*, pp. 440–1.

14 Irvin D. Yalom, *Staring at The Sun. Overcoming the Terror of Death*, Wiley, San Francisco 2009, p. 12.

15 Jan Assmann, *Cultural Memory and Early Civilization*, p. 19.

16 Elias Canetti, *Il libro contro la morte* [*The Book Against Death*], p. 271.

17 Walter Benjamin, *Central Park*, New German Critique, no. 34 (Winter 1985), pp. 48–9.

18 James Joyce, *Ulysses*, Wordsworth Editions, 2010, p. 102. See also *Voices of the Dead*, Phonoscope, 1896, n. 1.

19 See Guy Debord, *Society of the Spectacle*, Zone Books, Princeton NJ 1994.

20 Plato, *Phaedrus*, 275d–76a.

21 John Durham Peters, *Speaking into the Air. A History of the Idea of Communication*, University of Chicago Press, Chicago IL 1999, p. 152.

22 Philippe Ariès, 'The Reversal of Death: Changes in Attitudes Toward Death in Western Societies', *American Quarterly*, 26 (5), Special Issue: Death in America (December 1974), p. 537.

23 Ibid., p. 548. On the changes to our relationship with death, see Davide Sisto, *Narrare la morte. Dal romanticismo al*

post-umano [*Narrating Death. From Romanticism to the Post-Human Era*], ETS, Pisa 2013.

24 Julian Huxley, *New Bottles for New Wine*, Chatto & Windus, London 1957, pp. 13–17. For more on this, see F. Ferrando, *Il Postumanesimo Filosofico e le Sue Alterità* [*Post-Humanism and Its Alterity*], ETS, Pisa 2017, p. 33.

25 Ruth Klüger, *Still Alive: A Holocaust Girlhood Remembered*, CUNY 2001. The quote is taken from Aleida Assmann, *Cultural Memory and Western Civilization*, p. 157.

26 See Roberto Manzocco, *Transhumanism. Engineering the Human Condition. History, Philosophy and Current Status*, Springer Praxis, Chichester 2019, pp. 113–30.

27 See Ray Kurzweil, *The Singularity is Near: When Humans Transcend Biology*, Viking, 2005, p. 320.

28 James Hughes, 'The Future of Death: Cryonics and the Telos of Liberal Democracy', *Journal of Evolution and Technology*, 6 (1), 2001; cited in Guy Brown, *The Living End: The Future of Death, Aging and Immortality*, p. 118.

29 Cited in Guy Brown, *The Living End: The Future of Death, Aging and Immortality*, p. 129.

30 Francesca A. Miglietti, *Identità mutanti* [*Mutant Identities*], op.cit., p. 52.

31 See Davide Sisto, *Online Afterlives*, op. cit., pp. 33–69.

32 Aleida Assmann, *Sette modi di dimenticare* [*Seven Ways of Forgetting*], op. cit., p. 21.

33 Jorge Luis Borges, *Funes the Memorious*, in *Labyrinths*, Penguin Classics 2000, p. 91.

34 Ibid., pp. 91–2.

35 Ibid., p. 92.

36 A.R. Luria, *The Mind of a Mnemonist: A Little Book about a Vast Memory*, Harvard University Press 1986.

37 Jorge Luis Borges, *Funes the Memorious*, p. 92.

38 Friedrich Nietzsche, *On the Utility and Liability of History for Life (1874)* in *The Nietzsche Reader* (eds Keith Ansell Pearson, Duncan Large), Blackwell, Oxford 2006, p. 127.

39 Elias Canetti, *The Agony of Flies*, Farrar, Straus and Giroux 1994.

40 Aleida Assmann, *Sette modi di dimenticare* [*Seven Ways of Forgetting*], op. cit., p. 9.

41 William James, *Principles of Psychology. Volumes 1–2*, Pantianos Classics, p. 285.

42 Viktor Mayer-Schönberger, *Delete. The Virtue of Forgetting in the Digital Age*, Princeton University Press, Princeton NJ 2009, p. 13.

43 Mark Fisher, *Ghosts of My Life. Writings on Depression, Hauntology and Lost Futures*, op. cit., p. 77.
44 For more on *flashbulb memories* see: R. Brown and J. Kulik, 'Flashbulb Memories', *Cognition*, 5 (1), 1977, 73–99; C. Finkenauer, O. Luminet, L. Gisle, El-Ahmad and M. van der Linden, 'Flashbulb Memories and the Underlying Mechanisms of their Formation: Toward an Emotional-Integrative Model', *Memory and Cognition* 26, 1998, 516–31. Available online is a clear description of the phenomenon, in M. Aricò, 'Emozione e memoria: le Flashbulb memories' [Emotion and Memory: Flashbulb Memories] in *State of Mind. Il Giornale delle scienze psicologiche* [*State of Mind. Journal of Psychological Sciences*], published 13 January 2016. https://www.stateofmind. it/2016/01/flashbulb-memories/
45 Jonathan Crary, 24/7. *Late Capitalism and the Ends of Sleep*, Verso, London 2014, pp. 10–11.
46 Ibid., p. 13.
47 Ibid., p. 34.
48 Mark Fisher, *Capitalist Realism. Is There No Alternative?*, Zero Books 2009, p. 54.
49 For a careful historical reconstruction of the meaning of melancholy, see in particular the following texts: Raymond Klibansky, Erwin Panofsky and Fritz Saxl, *Saturn and Melancholy: Studies in the History of Natural Philosophy, Religion and Art*, McGill-Queen's University Press 2019; Jean Starobinski, *History of the Treatment of Melancholy from the Earliest Times to 1900*, J.R. Geigy, 1962; Maurizio Calvesi, *La melanconia di Albrecht Dürer* [*Melancholy by Albrecht Dürer*], Einaudi, Turin 1993. I would also direct you to my book, *Lo specchio e il talismano. Schelling e la malinconia della natura* [*The Mirror and the Talisman. Schelling and the Melancholy of Nature*], AlboVersorio, Milan 2009.
50 E. Borgna, *Malinconia* [*Melancholy*], Feltrinelli, Milan 2001, p. 44.
51 Mark Fisher, *Capitalist Realism*, p. 21.
52 On this subject I would recommend watching the talk given by Valentino Megale at TedxDarsena in Milan (in Italian), entitled *Esperienze virtuali per cambiamenti reali* [*Virtual Experiences for Real Change*]. https://www.youtube.com/watch?v=Ny_oOsrKzgs. Valentino Megale is the co-founder of Softcare Studios, a startup focused on developing innovative solutions featuring virtual reality and artificial intelligence in order to provide psychological support for patients during treatment.
53 Simon Reynolds, *Retromania*, p. 62.

54 Mark Fisher, *Capitalist Realism*, pp. 9–10.
55 Simon Reynolds, *Retromania*, p. 63.
56 There is a splendid description of this particular experience in V.S. Naipaul's book *A Bend in the River*, which obviously adheres to the narrative taking place. Indar thinks the aeroplane is a marvellous thing, because it is faster than the heart. You can get to another place so quickly that you still feel like you are in the one you have left. You arrive in an instant, and leave in an instant, so there is no actual time in which to grow sad. 'And there is something else about the airplane. You can go back many times to the same place. And something strange happens if you go back often enough. You stop grieving for the past. You see that the past is something in your mind alone, that doesn't exist in real life. You trample on the past, you crush it. In the beginning it is like trampling on a garden. In the end you are just walking on ground. That is the way we have to learn to live now.' V.S. Naipaul, *A Bend in the River*, Pan Macmillan 2002, pp. 130–1.

Conclusion. Digital Inheritance and a Return to Oblivion

1 W.G. Sebald, *Campo Santo*, trans. Anthea Bell, Penguin, London 2013.
2 Vladimir Jankélévitch, *La morte* [*Death*], ed. E. Lisciani Petrini, Einaudi, Turin 2009, p. 390. For the French original, see *La mort*, Flammarion 2017.

Bibliography

Anders Günther, *Die Antiquiertheit des Menschen Bd 1: Über die Seele im Zeitalter der zweiten industriellen Revolution* [*The Outdatedness of Human Beings 1. On the Soul in the Era of the Second Industrial Revolution*], C.H. Beck, Munich 2018.

Arcagni Simone, *Visioni digitali. Video, web e nuove tecnologie* [*Digital Visions. Videos, Internet and New Technologies*], Einaudi, Turin 2017.

Arcagni Simone, *L'occhio della macchina* [*The Eye of the Machine*], Einaudi, Turin 2018.

Ardvidsson Adam and Delfanti Alessandro, *Introduction to Digital Media*, John Wiley & Sons, New Jersey 2019.

Ariès Philippe, *Western Attitudes Toward Death from the Middle Ages to the Present*, trans. Patricia Ranum, Johns Hopkins University Press, Baltimore MD 1974.

Ariès Philippe, 'The Reversal of Death: Changes in Attitudes Toward Death in Western Societies', *American Quarterly*, 26 (5), Special Issue: Death in America (December 1974), 536–60.

Arnold M., Gibbs M., Kohn T., Meese J. and Nansen B., *Death and Digital Media*, Routledge, London 2018.

Assmann Aleida, *Cultural Memory and Western Civilization: Functions, Media, Archives*. Cambridge University Press, Cambridge 2013.

Assmann Aleida, *Sette modi di dimenticare* [*Seven Ways of Forgetting*], Il Mulino, Bologna 2019.

Assmann Jan, *Cultural Memory and Early Civilization. Writing,*

Remembrance, and Political Imagination, Cambridge University Press, New York 2012.

Augé Marc, *The Future*, Verso, London 2014.

Barabási, Albert-Laszlo, *Linked*, Basic Books, New York 2014.

Baricco Alessandro, *The Game*, Einaudi, Turin 2018.

Barthes Roland, *Camera Lucida. Reflections on Photography*, trans. Richard Howard, Hill and Wang, New York 1981.

Bassett D.J., 'Who Wants to Live Forever? Living, Dying and Grieving in Our Digital Society', *Social Sciences*, 4 (4), 2015, 1127–39.

Baudrillard Jean, *Symbolic Exchange and Death*, SAGE, London 2014.

Bauman Zygmunt, *Mortality, Immortality and Other Life Strategies*, Polity, Cambridge 2013.

Bazzichelli Tatiana, *Networking. The Net as Artwork*, Digital Aesthetics Research Centre, Aarhus University, Aarhus 2008.

Bell Gordon and Gemmell Jim, *Total Recall. How the E-Memory Revolution Will Change Everything*, E.P. Dutton and Co., Boston MA 2009.

Belting Hans, *An Anthropology of Images: Picture, Medium, Body*, Princeton University Press, Princeton NJ 2011.

Benasayag Miguel and Schmit Gérard, *Les passions tristes. Souffrance psychique et crise sociale*, La Découverte, Paris 2006.

Benjamin Walter, *Angelus Novus. Saggi e frammenti*, Einaudi, Turin 2014. This collection has no direct equivalent in English translation. However, most if not all of its contents are readily available in English.

Bentivegna Sara and Boccia Artieri Giovanni, *Le teorie delle comunicazioni di massa e la sfida digitale* [*Theories of Mass Communication and the Digital Challenge*], Laterza, Rome-Bari 2019.

Berardi (Bifo) Franco, *Futurability. The Age of Impotence and the Horizon of Possibility*, Verso, London 2019.

Berardi (Bifo) Franco, *After the Future*, AK Press, Chico CA 2011.

Bergson Henri, *Matter and Memory*, CreateSpace Independent Publishing Platform, 2016.

Boccia Artieri Giovanni, *Gli effetti sociali del Web. Forme della comunicazione e metodologie della ricerca online* [*The Social Effects of the Internet. Forms of Communication and Methodologies of Online Research*], Franco Angeli, Milan 2015.

Bolter Jay David and Grusin Richard, *Remediation: Understanding New Media*, MIT Press, Cambridge MA 2000.

Boni Stefano, *Homo comfort. Il superamento tecnologico della fatica e le sue conseguenze* [*Homo Comfort. Technology's Defeat of Hard Work, and its Consequences*], Elèuthera, Milan 2014.

Boyd D. and Ellison N.B., 'Social Network Sites: Definition, History, and Scholarship', *Journal of Computer-Mediated Communication*, 13 (1), 2007, 210–30.

Braman J., Dudley A. and Valenti G., 'Death, Social Networks and Virtual Worlds: A Look into the Digital Afterlife', in *Proceedings of the 9th ACIS Conference on Software Engineering Research, Management and Applications (SERA 2011)*,Washington (DC), 2011, pp. 186–92.

Brecht Bertolt, *In Praise of Forgetting*, in *The Collected Poems of Bertolt Brecht*, trans. and ed. David Constantine, Tom Kuhn, W.W. Norton and Company, London 2018.

Bridle James, *New Dark Age. Technology and the End of Future*, Verso, London 2019.

Brown G., *The Living End: The Future of Death, Aging and Immortality*, Macmillan Science 2007.

Brubaker J., 'Beyond the Grave: Facebook as a Site for the Expansion of Death and Mourning', *The Information Society*, 29, 2013, 152–63.

Brubaker J.R. and Vertesi J., 'Death and the Social Network'. Paper presented at the CHI 2010 Workshop on the subject *HCI at the End of Life: Understanding Death, Dying, and the Digital*, Atlanta, GA. http://www.dgp.toronto.edu/~mikem/hcieol/subs/brubaker.pdf.

Caffo Leonardo, *Obbligati alla nostalgia. Gli algoritmi dei social network e il male d'archivio* [*Bound to Nostalgia. Social Network Algorithms and Archive Fever*], *L'Espresso*, cultural insert of *La Repubblica*, Anno LXIV, n.51 (16 December 2018), 83–4.

Canetti Elias, *Das Buch gegen den Tod*, Hanser Verlag, Munich 2014.

Cann Candi K., *Virtual Afterlives: Grieving the Dead in the Twenty-First Century*, University Press of Kentucky, Lexington KY 2014.

Carbone Mauro, *Filosofia-schermi. Dal cinema alla rivoluzione digitale* [*Screen Philosophy: From Cinema to the Digital Revolution*], Cortina, Milan 2016.

Carroll Evan and Romano John, *Your Digital Afterlife. When Facebook, Flickr and Twitter Are Your Estate, What's Your Legacy?*, New Riders, Berkeley CA 2011.

Castells Manuel, *The Internet Galaxy: Reflections on the Internet, Business, and Society*, Oxford University Press, Oxford 2002.

Castells Manuel, *The Rise of the Network Society*, Wiley-Blackwell, Chichester 2010.

Codeluppi Vanni, *La vetrinizzazione sociale. Il processo di spettaco-larizzazione degli individui e della società* [*Social Shop Windows. The Process of Spectacularization of Individuals and Society*], Bollati Boringhieri, Turin 2007.

Crary Jonathan, *24/7. Late Capitalism and the Ends of Sleep*, Verso, London 2014.

Debord Guy, *The Society of the Spectacle*, Zone Books, Princeton NJ 1994.

DeGroot D., 'Keeping Our People Alive: The Role of Digital Immortality in Culture Preservation', in T. Dreier and E. Euler (eds), *Kulturelles Gedächtnis im 21. Jahrhundert. Tagungsband des internationalen Symposiums*, 23 April 2005, Karlsruhe, Universitätsverlag Karlsruhe, Karlsruhe 2005, pp. 33–56.

De Maria Giorgio, *The Twenty Days of Turin: A Novel*, trans. Roland Glazov, Liveright, New York 2017.

Derrida Jacques, *Archive Fever. A Freudian Impression*, University of Chicago Press, Chicago IL 1998.

Derrida Jacques, *Specters of Marx: The State of the Debt, the Work of Mourning and the New International*, Routledge, Abingdon 2006.

Derrida Jacques, *The End of the World and Other Teachable Moments*, Fordham University Press, New York 2014.

Deuze Mark, *Media Life*, Polity, Cambridge 2012.

Dominici Piero, *Dentro la società interconnessa. Prospettive etiche per un nuovo ecosistema della comunicazione* [*Inside the Interconnected Society. Ethical Perspectives for a New Communication Ecosystem*], FrancoAngeli, Milan 2019.

Eco Umberto, *La memoria vegetale e altri scritti di bibliofilia* [*The Vegetal Memory and Other Writings on Bibliophilia*], La Nave di Teseo, Milan 2018.

Eichhorn Kate, *The End of Forgetting. Growing Up With Social Media*, Harvard University Press, Cambridge MA 2019.

Fechner Gustav Theodor, *The Little Book of Life after Death*, RedWheelWeiser, Boston PA 2005.

Ferraris Maurizio, *Documentality. Why It is Necessary to Leave Traces*, Fordham University Press, New York 2012.

Finn Ed, *What Algorithms Want. Imagination in the Age of Computing*, MIT Press, Cambridge MA 2018.

Fisher Mark, *Capitalist Realism. Is There No Alternative?*, Zero Books 2009.

Fisher Mark, *Ghosts of My Life. Writings on Depression, Hauntology and Lost Futures*, Zero Books 2014.

Fisher Mark, *The Weird and the Eerie*, Repeater Books, London 2016.

Floridi Luciano, *The Fourth Revolution. How the Infosphere is Reshaping Human Reality*, Oxford University Press, Oxford 2014.

Flusser, Vilém, *Into the Universe of Technical Images*, University of Minnesota Press, Minnesota MN 2011.

Fontcuberta Joan, *La furia de las imágenes. Notas sobre la postfotografía*, Galaxia Gutenberg, Barcelona 2017.

Garde-Hansen J., Hoskins A. and Reading A. (eds), *Save As … Digital Memories*, Palgrave Macmillan, New York 2009.

Gardner Howard and Davis Katie, *The App Generation: How Today's Youth Navigate Identity, Intimacy and Imagination in a Digital World*, Yale University Press, New Haven CT 2013.

Gawande Atul, *Being Mortal. Medicine and What Matters in the End*, Profile Books, London 2015.

Gheno Vera, *Da nativi a 'disagiati digitali': nuovi analfabetismi crescono online* [*From Natives to the 'Digitally Impaired': New Forms of Illiteracy Grow Online*, in *Agenda digitale*, 17 October 2019. https://www.agendadigitale.eu/cultura-digitale/da-nativi-a-disagiati-digitali-nuovi-analfabetismi-emergono-online/.

Gheno Vera and Mastroianni Bruno, *Tienilo acceso! Posta, commenta, condividi senza spegnere il cervello* [*Keep it on! Post, Comment, Share Without Switching off Your Brain*], Longanesi, Milan 2018.

Gleick James, *Faster: The Acceleration of Just About Everything*, Little Brown and Company, London 1999.

Gnoli V., Marino L. and Rosati M., *Organizzare la conoscenza. Dalle biblioteche all'architettura dell'informazione per il Web* [*Organizing Knowledge. From Libraries to Information Architecture for the Internet*], Tecniche Nuove, Milan 2006.

Goldsmith Kenneth, *Uncreative Writing. Managing Language in the Digital Age*, Columbia University Press, New York 2011.

Goldsmith Kenneth, *Wasting Time on the Internet*, HarperCollins, New York 2016.

Gottschall Jonathan, *The Storytelling Animal: How Stories Make Us Human*, Houghton Mifflin Harcourt, New York 2012.

Gray S.E., 'The Memory Remains: Visible Presences within the Network', *Thanatos*, 3 (1), 2014.

Han, Byung-Chul, *The Transparency Society*, Stanford University Press, Stanford 2015.

Han Byung-Chul, *Psychopolitics: Neoliberalism and New Technologies of Power*, Verso, London 2017.

Han, Byung-Chul, *In the Swarm. Digital Prospects*, MIT Press, Cambridge MA 2017.

Han Byung-Chul, *The Expulsion of the Other: Society, Perception and Communication Today*, trans. Wieland Hoban, Polity, Cambridge 2018.

Harari Yuval Noah, *Homo Deus. A Brief History of Tomorrow*, Random House, London 2016.

Haverinen, A., 'Actual(ly) Mourning: Using Autoethnography in Virtual Mourning Research', paper presented at the Death and Media Symposium, Helsinki Collegium for Advanced Studies, 06/06/2013. https://www.academia.edu/4382651/ Actually_mourning_Haverinen.

Hobbs R. William and Burke K. Moira, 'Connective Recovery in Social Networks After the Death of a Friend', *Nature Human Behaviour*, 1 (2017). https://www.nature.com/articles/ s41562-017-0092.

Iaconesi Salvatore and Persico Oriana, *La cura* [*The Cure*], Codice, Turin 2016.

Jacobsen M.H. (ed.), *Postmortal Society. Towards a Sociology of Immortality*, Routledge, London 2017.

Jankélévitch Vladimir, *La mort*, Flammarion, 2017.

Jimroglou Krissi M., 'A Camera with a View: JenniCAM, Visual Representation and Cyborg Subjectivity', *Information, Communication and Society*, 2 (4), 1999, 439–53.

Kasket Elaine, 'Continuing Bonds in the Age of Social Networking: Facebook as a Modern-Day Medium', *Bereavement Care*, 31 (2), 2012, 62–9.

Kasket Elaine, *All the Ghosts in the Machine. Illusions of Immortality in the Digital Age*, Robinson, London 2019.

Keen Andrew, *Digital Vertigo: How Today's Online Social Revolution is Dividing, Diminishing and Disorienting Us*, Constable, London 2012.

Kelly Kevin, *The Inevitable. Understanding the 12 Technological Forces That Will Shape Our Future*, Penguin, New York 2017.

Kiš Danilo, *Encyclopedia of the Dead*, Northwestern University Press, Evanston IL 1997.

Klass D. and Steffen E.M. (eds), *Continuing Bonds in Bereavement*, Routledge, London 2018.

Klass D., Silverman P. and Nickman S., *Continuing Bonds: New Understandings of Grief (Death Education, Aging and Health Care)*, Taylor & Francis, Bristol 1996.

Kovalsky Robin M. and McCord A., 'If I Knew Then What I Know Now: Advice to My Younger Self', *Journal of Social Psychology*, 5 May 2019. https://www.tandfonline.com/doi/full/10.1080/002 24545.2019.1609401.

Lagerkvist A., 'New Memory Cultures and Death: Existential Security in the Digital Memory Ecology', *Thanatos*, 2 (2), 2013.

Lanier Jaron, *Dawn of the New Everything: A Journey Through Virtual Reality*, Il Saggiatore, Milan 2019.

Lanier Jaron, *Ten Arguments for Deleting Your Social Media Accounts Right Now*, Vintage 2019.

Lejeune Philippe, *Le pacte autobiographique*, Éditions du Seuil, Paris 1997.

Lévy Pierre, *Becoming Virtual. Reality in the Digital Age*, Perseus Books, New York 1998.

Maciel C. and Carvalho Pereira V. (eds), *Digital Legacy and Interaction. Post-Mortem Issues*, Springer, New York 2013.

McIlwain, C., *When Death Goes Pop: Death, Media and the Remaking of Community*, Peter Lang, New York 2005.

Magnusson M., *The Gentle Art of Swedish Death Cleaning. How to Free Yourself and Your Family from a Lifetime of Clutter*, Simon & Schuster, New York 2018.

Maldonado Tomás, *Memoria y concimiento: Sobre los destinos del saber en la perspectiva digital* [*Memory and Knowledge. On the Fate of Knowledge in Digital Perspective*], Gedisa Editorial, Barcelona 2007.

Malone Michael S., *The Guardian of All Things: The Epic Story of Human Memory*, St Martin's Press, New York 2012.

Manovich Lev, *The Language of New Media*, MIT Press, Cambridge MA 2002.

Marchesini Roberto, *Post-human. Verso nuovi modelli di esistenza*, Bollati Boringhieri, Turin 2002. / *Beyond Anthropocentrism. Thoughts for a Post-Human Philosophy*, Mimesis International, Milan 2018.

Martinelli Silvia, *Diritti all'oblio e motori di ricerca. Memoria e privacy nell'era digitale* [*The Right to be Forgotten and Search Engines. Memory and Privacy in the Digital Era*], Giuffré Editore, Milan 2017.

Massimi M. and Charise A., 'Dying, Death and Mortality: Towards Thanatosensitivity' in *HCI*, CHI 2009, 4–9 April, Boston MA 2009.

Mayer-Schönberger Viktor, *Delete. The Virtue of Forgetting in the Digital Age*, Princeton University Press, Princeton NJ 2009.

Mayer-Schönberger Viktor and Cukier Kenneth, *Big Data. A Revolution that Will Transform How We Live, Work and Think*, John Murray Publishers, 2013.

Mazzocco Davide, *Cronofagia. Come il capitalismo depreda il nostro tempo* [*Chronophagia. How Capitalism Deprives Us of Our Time*], D. Editore, Rome 2018.

Meese J., Gibbs M. and Carter M. et al., 'Selfies at Funerals: Mourning and Presencing on Social Media Platforms', *International Journal of Communication*, 9 (2015), 1818–31.

Miglietti F.A., *Identità mutanti. Dalla piega alla piaga: esseri delle contaminazioni contemporanee* [*Mutant Identities*], Mondadori, Milan 2004.

Moreman C.M. and Lewis A.D. (eds), *Digital Death: Mortality and Beyond in the Online Age*, Praeger, Westport CT 2014.

Nietzsche Friedrich, *On the Utility and Liability of History for Life (1874)* in *The Nietzsche Reader* (eds Keith Ansell Pearson, Duncan Large), Blackwell, Oxford 2006.

O'Connell Mark, *To Be a Machine: Adventures Among Cyborgs, Utopians, Hackers and the Futurists Solving the Modest Problem of Death*, Granta, London 2017.

Paccagnella L. and Vellar A., *Vivere online. Identità, relazioni, conoscenza,* [*Living Online. Identities, Relationships, Knowledge*], Il Mulino, Bologna 2016.

Parisi Francesco, *La tecnologia che siamo* [*Technology and Us*], Codice, Turin 2019.

Pepperell Robert, *The Posthuman Condition: Consciousness Beyond the Brain*, University of Chicago Press, Chicago IL 1995.

Peters, John Durham, *Speaking into the Air: A History of the Idea of Communication,* University of Chicago Press, Chicago IL 1999.

Pinotti A. and Somaini A., *Cultura visuale. Immagini, sguardi, media, dispositivi* [*Visual Culture. Images, Gazes, Media, Devices*], Einaudi, Turin 2016.

Pitsillides, S., 2012, 'Transcending the Archive: Reflections on Online Identity and Death', paper presented at the international conference, 'Memento Mori: Technology Design for the End of Life', Austin, Texas, 6 May 2012.

Quintarelli Stefano, *Capitalismo immateriale. Le tecnologie digitali e il nuovo conflitto sociale* [*Immaterial Capitalism. Digital Technologies and the New Social Conflict*], Bollati Boringhieri, Turin 2019.

Quiroga Rodrigo Quian, *Borges and Memory. Encounters with the Human Brain*, Erickson, Trento 2018.

Reynolds Simon, *Retromania. A Pop Culture's Addiction to Its Own Past*, Faber and Faber, London 2011.

Rheingold H., *The Virtual Community: Homesteading on the Electronic Frontier*, Addison-Wesley, Boston MA 1993.

Riva Giuseppe, *I social network* [*The Social Networks*], Il Mulino, Bologna 2016.

Riva Giuseppe, *Selfie. Narcisismo e identità* [*Selfie. Narcissism and Identity*], Il Mulino, Bologna 2016.

Ross Alec, *The Industries of the Future*, Simon & Schuster, London 2016.

Rossi Paolo, *Il passato, la memoria, l'oblio* [*The Past, Memory, Forgetting*], Il Mulino, Bologna 1991.

Rothblatt M., *Virtually Human: The Promise – and the Peril – of Digital Immortality*, St Martin's Press, New York 2014.

Rumsey S. Abby, *When We Are No More. How Digital Memory Is Shaping Our Future*, Bloomsbury Press, New York 2016.

Rushkoff Douglas, *Present Shock. When Everything Happens Now*, Penguin, New York 2013.

Sadin é, *La silicolonisation du monde: L'irrésistible expansion du libéralisme numérique* [*The Siliconization of the World. The Irresistible Expansion of Digital Liberalism*] Éditions L'Échappée 2016.

Schelling F.W.J., *The Ages of the World*, SUNY, New York 2000.

Schelling F.W.J., *Clara, Or on Nature's Connection to the Spirit World*, SUNY, New York 2002.

Sherlock A., 'Larger Than Life: Digital Resurrection and the Re-Enchantment of Society', *The Information Society: An International Journal*, 29 (3), 2013, 164–76.

Sisto Davide, *Narrare la morte. Dal romanticismo al post-umano* [*Narrating Death. From Romanticism to the Post-Human Era*], ETS, Pisa 2013.

Sisto Davide, *Online Afterlives: Immortality, Memory, and Grief in Digital Culture*, MIT Press, Cambridge MA 2020.

Sloane D.C., *Is the Cemetery Dead?*, University of Chicago Press, Chicago IL 2018.

Sofka C., 'Social Support "Internetworks", Caskets for Sale, and More: Thanatology and the Information Superhighway', *Death Studies*, 21 (6), 1997, 553–74.

Sontag Susan, *On Photography*, Penguin Random House, London, 2019.

Sozzi Marina, *Non sono il mio tumore. Curarsi il cancro in Italia* [*I Am Not My Tumour. Being Treated for Cancer in Italy*], Chiarelettere, Milan 2019.

Spitzer Manfred, *Einsamkeit: Die unerkannte Krankheit* [*Loneliness. The Silent Epidemic*], Droemer Verlag, Munich 2018.

Steinhart E.C., *Your Digital Afterlives: Computational Theories of Life after Death*, Palgrave Macmillan, New York 2014.

Tarpino Antonella, *Geografie della memoria. Case, rovine, oggetti quotidiani* [*Geographies of Memory. Houses, Ruins, Daily Objects*], Einaudi, Turin 2008.

Tomasin Lorenzo, *L'impronta digitale. Cultura umanistica e tecnologia* [*Digital Footprint*], Carocci, Rome 2017.

Turkle Sherry, *Reclaiming Conversation: The Power of Talk in a Digital Age*, Penguin, New York 2015.

Turkle Sherry, *Alone Together. Why We Expect More from Technology and Less from Each Other*, Basic Books, New York 2011.

Veale K., 'Online Memorialisation: The Web as a Collective Memorial Landscape for Remembering the Dead' in *Fibreculture*, 3, 2004. http://three.fibreculturejournal.org/fcj-014-online-memorialisation-the-web-as-a-collective-memorial-landscape-for-remembering-the-dead/.

Vlahos J., *Talk to me. Amazon, Google, Apple and the Race for Voice-Controlled AI*, Random House, London 2019.

Wallace Patricia, *The Psychology of the Internet*, Cambridge University Press, Cambridge 2012.

Walter T., 'A New Model of Grief. Bereavement and Biography', *Mortality*, 1 (1), 1996, 7–25.

Walter T., 'New mourners, old mourners. Online memorial culture as a chapter in the history of mourning', *New Review of Hypermedia and Multimedia*, 21(1–2), 2015, 10–24.

Walter T., 'Communication Media and the Dead: From the Stone Age to Facebook', *Mortality*, 20 (3), 2015, 215–32.

Walter T., 'The Dead Who Become Angels: Bereavement and Vernacular Religion', *Omega*, 73, 2016, 3–28.

Walter T., 'The Pervasive Dead', *Mortality*, 2018, 1–16.

Walter T., Hourizi R., Moncur W. and Pitsillides S., 'Does the Internet Change How We Die and Mourn?', *Omega*, 64 (4), 2011–12, 275–302.

Warburton S. and Hatzipanagos S. (eds), *Digital Identity and Social Media*, IGI Global, Hershey PA 2013.

Ziccardi Giovanni, *Il libro digitale dei morti. Memoria, lutto, eternità e oblio nell'era dei social network* [*The Digital Book of the Dead. Memory, Grief, Eternity and Oblivion in the Age of Social Networks*], Utet, Turin 2017.

Ziccardi Giovanni, *Tecnologie del potere. Come usare i social network in politica* [*Technologies of Power. How to use Social Networks in Politics*], Cortina, Milan 2019.

Index